WEIMAR
EYEWITNESS

The burning Reichstag – February 27–28, 1933

WEIMAR
EYEWITNESS

Egon Larsen

Bachman & Turner
London

Books by the same author

Men Who Changed the World, Phoenix (Dents) & Roy, New York, 1952.

An American in Europe: Count Rumford, Rider & Philos. Libr., N.Y., 1953.

The Young Traveller in Germany, Phoenix & Dutton, N.Y., 1954.

Atomic Energy: The First Hundred Years, Harrap & Pan Books, 1958.

A History of Invention, Phoenix & Roy, 1961.

The Cavendish Laboratory: Nursery of Genius, Edward Ward, 1962.

Laughter in a Damp Climate: Anthology of British Humour, Jenkins & Arco, New York, 1963.

The Deceivers: Lives of the Great Impostors, John Baker & Roy, 1966.

Munich (Cities of the World Series), Phoenix & Roy, 1967.

Great Humorous Stories of the World, Arthur Baker, 1967.

First with the Truth: Newspapermen in Action, John Baker & Roy, 1968.

One Man Against Napoleon: Carlo-Andrea Pozzo di Borgo, Dobson, 1968.

Strange Sects and Cults, Arthur Baker & Hart, New York, 1971.

Motives (Anthol., Contemporary German Authors; transl & introd.), Oswald Wolff, 1975.

Bachman & Turner
45 Calthorpe Street
London WC1X 0HH

ISBN 0 85974 051 X
First published 1976
Photoset by *The Benham Press*, Colchester, Essex.

CONTENTS

ACKNOWLEDGEMENTS

Author and publisher wish to express their thanks to the Wiener Library, London, for its invaluable help in compiling this book; to Jonathan Cape Ltd., London for permission to publish translations of Erich Kästner's poems; and to the following for supplying photographs:
National Film Archive, London (pp. 25, 137)
Süddeutscher Verlag, Munich (pp. 59, 87, 169, 181)
Keystone Press Agency, London (pp. 167, 179)
Fox Photos, London (Frontispiece)
Atrium Verlag, Zurich (p. 100)

1
ATTENTION – FIRING STARTS NOW

The cuirassier's outfit which I had been given for my tenth birthday came in handy two weeks later. With my tin sword drawn, I stood to attention at the door of our block of flats in Munich, paying my respects to the field-grey columns of soldiers in their spiked helmets as they marched off to the front under a blazing August sun, singing and with roses stuck in their rifle muzzles.

Four years and three months later, things looked very different. We were cold and hungry, the summer sky had turned into melancholy, leaden, dripping clouds, and the patriotic youngster into a fervently revolutionary lad. I felt and prayed that our town would soon be the scene of some great historical event; it did not disappoint me. After the prelude of a naval mutiny at Kiel in the first days of November, 1918, the German revolution which ended the war began at Munich.

There were some good reasons. For our town, probably more than for any other provincial capital in Germany, the war had been catastrophic. Munich and its particular way of life had been largely shaped by two extravagant, art-crazy, cranky Bavarian kings (one had drowned himself, and his successor was so mad that a Prince Regent had to rule in his place). But the town had a solid, almost rustic middle-class which was the backbone of its society, with strong ties to the countryside and the mountains – you can see the Alps on a clear day, but you feel their mighty presence all the time, and down from the Alps comes the *Föhn,* a warm south wind probably originating in the Sahara. It has curious results for the people, causing lassitude, irritability, moodiness, introspection, but it also seems to sharpen artistic sensitivity. That, no less than the Bavarian kings' attitude, probably encouraged the growth of a colony of artists in the suburb of Schwabing – Munich's Hampstead or

Greenwich Village: painters, writers, intellectuals, and general Bohemians. Their presence at the fringe of the town provided a little spice and levity and imaginative excitement for a society that often tended to be half asleep.

The war had destroyed Munich's characteristic bourgeois-rustic-Bohemian atmosphere, its quiet, unambitious *Gemütlichkeit* and tolerance. Like most highlanders, the Bavarians put up patiently with a lot of hardship, reacting with no more than a bit of their habitual grumbling. But when some unpredictable limit has been reached there comes a flashpoint, their temper suddenly quickens, their blood begins to boil, and the great fracas starts. Still, considering the potential violence of the exasperated people of Munich, the rising of Wednesday, November 7, 1918 — two days before the Berlin revolution — went off in quite an orderly manner, thanks to its leader.

A mass meeting had been called by the two Socialist parties, the Social Democrats and the Independent Social Democrats, on the Theresienwiese (in peace time the site of the famous October Festival). About a hundred thousand men and women — one sixth of the town's population — assembled early in the afternoon of that Wednesday. The main speaker, and the most effective one, was not a Bavarian but a bearded, bespectacled, fifty-year-old Jewish intellectual from Berlin by the name of Kurt Eisner.

In social terms, Munich was still a small town where everybody knew everybody else. We all knew who Kurt Eisner was. The son of a well-to-do manufacturer of army equipment, he had studied philosophy and, as a result, become a radical Socialist, a pacifist, and an implacable enemy of the reactionary, chauvinist Prussian establishment that dominated Imperial Germany. At 30, Eisner went to prison in Berlin for the first time, sentenced to nine months for writing a critical article about the Kaiser. In 1910 he settled in Munich, where he was soon a familiar figure in the cafés of the literati. At first he wrote and worked for the Social-Democratic Party, but its support of the war disgusted him, and in 1917 he became chief publicist of the newly formed Independent Social-Democratic Party, which was to play an important role in the revolution and the early days of the German Republic. The Independents were the reddest sector in the Bavarian political spectrum — there was no Communist

Party yet, and its forerunner, the Spartacus League, had only just been set up in Berlin.

Now in his middle age, Kurt Eisner was a friendly, selfless, and unassuming man, despite his great gifts as an orator. He was completely devoted to his political ideals — peace (which included non-violence) and social justice. Unfortunately, he had an *idée fixe* which, before long, was to prove fatal for him. He believed that Germany would have to admit that she was guilty of causing the war, in order to get tolerable armistice conditions from the Allies, and as a sincere contribution to world peace. He put his trust in President Wilson and his famous 'Fourteen Points' of January, 1918, the statement of Allied war and peace aims, including the concept of a League of Nations.

With his insistence on Germany's admission of her war guilt, Eisner made the same mistake as other political intellectuals by ignoring the German national character to which the idea of crying *peccavi* has always been obnoxious. In his pacifist fervour Eisner went so far as to 'edit' — some said fake — a number of documents allegedly proving Germany's war guilt.

Early in 1918, he went to prison for another spell of nine months for calling the workers in a number of Bavarian towns out on strike. Released in mid-October, he threw himself passionately into the struggle for ending the war, overthrowing the monarchy, and turning Bavaria — and, if possible, all Germany — into a democratic society. That was the gist of his great speech before the one hundred thousand people who had gathered on the Theresienwiese. He and the other speakers from the Social-Democratic Party told them to march through the town and set up workers' and soldiers' councils which were to seize power in Munich.

An enormous procession formed, picking up sympathizers on the way. I had just finished my private cramming lessons in Latin and Greek with one of my grammar-school teachers, and met the demonstrators on my way home in one of the wide thoroughfares of the town. They were marching ten or fifteen abreast, with red banners and makeshift posters, shouting 'Peace', 'Long live the revolution', and 'Down with the dynasties' in rhythm with their tramping feet. I marched along with them on the sidewalk. Soldiers from the barracks went over to them — in one of the barracks the soldiers had been locked in by the military police and shouted out to the demonstrators to force open the doors. Many officers demonstratively tore off their own epaulets as they joined us. When we came to the bridge across the river Isar, which led to my home, the demonstrators seemed ready to disperse; I thought the fun was over, and I mustn't keep my parents waiting.

In fact, the marchers turned back to the government buildings, the Town Hall, and the newspaper offices, and occupied them all. There was practically no opposition. The old king had been taking his customary afternoon walk in the public park; a breathless court official ran after him and shouted the classic warning, 'Your Majesty, go home, there's a revolution!' And Ludwig III, the last of the Wittlesbach kings, went home to his palace, climbed with his queen into the motor-car that was already waiting for him at the back door, and drove to his farm in the country, never to return to Munich.

There was, of course, no school the next day; those of us pupils who had no bicycles could not have reached it anyway as the tramcars, the town's only means of public transport, had stopped running. But the elderly women who delivered all the town's morning papers did their job as usual. The whole front page was taken up by a proclamation telling us what had happened (a shorter version, printed on glaring red poster paper, had already been pasted on the walls during the night):

To the Population of Munich!

The terrible fate which struck the German people has led to an elemental movement of Munich's workers and soldiers. A provisional Workers', Soldiers', and Peasants' Council was formed in the *Landtag* [Bavarian Parliament] during the night preceding November 8.

From now on, Bavaria is a Free State.

A people's government, supported by the trust of the masses, will be set up immediately.

A legislative national assembly, for which all adult men and women are entitled to vote, will meet as soon as possible.

A new age is dawning!

Bavaria wants to make Germany ready for the League of Nations.

The democratic and social Republic of Bavaria has the moral power to secure for Germany a peace that saves her from the worst. The present rising was necessary for creating, without unduly violent disturbances, stable conditions before the enemy's armies surge across the borders, or the demobilized German troops cause chaos after the armistice.

The Workers', Soldiers', and Peasants' Council will safeguard strictest order. Excesses will be ruthlessly suppressed. The safety of person and property is guaranteed.

The soldiers in the barracks will govern themselves through the Soldiers' Councils, and maintain discipline. Officers who do not obstruct the demands of the changed circumstances shall be allowed to do their duty without hindrance.

We rely on the active assistance of the whole population. All who work for the new freedom are welcome. All civil servants remain in their positions. Basic social and political reforms will be initiated without delay.

The farmers guarantee the supply of food to the towns. The old antagonism between country and town will disappear. The distribution of foodstuffs will be organized effectively.

Workers and citizens of Munich! Put your trust in the great and mighty cause which is evolving in these fateful days!

Everyone must help to complete the unavoidable change quickly, easily, and peacefully.

In these times of wild, senseless slaughter we abhor all bloodshed. Every human life shall be sacred.

Keep calm and lend a hand to build a new world!

The fratricidal struggle among the Socialists has come to an end in Bavaria. The working masses are returning to unity on the revolutionary basis which now exists.

Long live the Bavarian Republic! Long live peace! Long live the creative work of the toiling masses!

Munich, *Landtag,* in the night preceding November 8, 1918.

THE COUNCIL OF THE WORKERS, SOLDIERS, AND PEASANTS
The Chairman: Kurt Eisner.

Eisner was justified in putting only his own name under that proclamation. He had written it, and it was his vision of the new State which he was conveying to us in a kind of poster-style shorthand, asking us to help him build it. He was an extraordinary character, a revolutionary leader who hated force and violence, and who begged the people to trust him.

On the afternoon of that Thursday, November 8 – Eisner had slept a few hours on a sofa in the *Landtag* building – a provisional National Council was set up, consisting of all those who happened to be around: soldiers' and workers' delegates, trade-unionists, Social-Democratic, Independent, and left-wing Liberal Members of the old Bavarian Parliament. The National Council elected a provisional government, of course with Eisner as the Premier; he also assumed the post of Foreign Minister. The Social-Democratic leader, Erhard Auer – next to Eisner the most important personality of the day – was appointed Minister of the Interior.

The revolution was over. Or was it?

Three months and two weeks later, on February 21, 1919, I stood at a street corner near the *Landtag,* staring at a large pool of blood that had been hastily covered with sand. I had rushed to the inner town straight from school; we had heard rumours that something dreadful had happened.

On that corner, Kurt Eisner had been shot dead by a young fanatic, Count Arco-Valley, the scion of an old Bavarian aristocratic family; he wanted to silence for ever the man who was proclaiming Germany's war guilt to the world. Eisner's bodyguard shot and wounded the murderer (who, by an irony of history, was himself murdered in one of Hitler's concentration camps two decades later).

Eisner had been on his way to the opening session of the new Bavarian Parliament after the elections of January, 1919. He carried in his pocket the text of his own and the provisional government's resignation according to democratic procedure so

12

that a new government could be formed on the basis of the strength of the parties. Thus, Bavaria would have started on the road to a solidly democratic political life. But instead of Eisner reading out his resignation, Erhard Auer opened the session, deeply shocked, with an impromptu obituary of 'the leader of the Bavarian revolution, a man filled with the purest idealism and sincere concern for the proletariat'. He had hardly finished his speech when a stranger pushed his way through to the ministerial rostrum, pulled out a pistol and fired some shots at Auer; then he turned round and shot madly into the hall. Auer was severely injured and had to retire from political life for years; two Members were killed outright. The stranger turned out to be a disgruntled butcher, a mental case.

Pandemonium broke lose in the town which had just begun to settle down after the tribulations of the war years. Within a few days the extremists, who now called themselves Spartacists and whom Eisner had managed to keep in check, gained the upper hand in Munich. A 'Central Council of the Bavarian Republic' replaced the government, proclaimed a general strike, put Munich in a 'state of siege', and ordered the censorship of the 'bourgeois' press. That was the second revolution, as we called it. The 'Republican Guard', an armed organization which had been set up by the Social Democrats, tried to stop it but failed. Thousands of troops who had returned from the front but refused to give up their rifles, hand grenades and machine-guns, backed the Workers' and Soldiers' Councils who exercised the physical power in the town, but without any political unity. 'Weapons have to be left in the cloakroom', said a notice on the doors of the beer-hall where the Councils held their first big rally.

There were many days without tramways. The typical scene in the main squares of Munich in March, 1919, was that of large and small groups of citizens and soldiers standing around the useless tram stops, endlessly discussing events, ruminating over rumours.

For some weeks we had two or more rival governments. One, which had managed to get itself elected by the *Landtag,* was composed of moderate and Independent Social Democrats; among its first actions was the abolition of Bavaria's nobility – a meaningless sop to the workers who were infuriated at Eisner's assassination by an aristocrat. Another ephemeral government,

13

shaky from the start because of the incessant personal and ideological quarrels among its members, was the *Zentralrat*, the Central Council of the Workers and Soldiers. Three dominant figures emerged in those days: the Russian-born, 'orthodox' Bolshevik Eugen Leviné, who was said to get his orders from Moscow, and the anarchists Erich Mühsam and Gustav Landauer, both intellectuals. Mühsam was well known in Schwabing as a satirical song writer and interpreter of his own works at the most famous literary cabaret, the *Simplicissimus*; he had published a few volumes of poems before the war. Landauer was a serious political theoretician and literary historian, who interrupted his work on a two-volume study of Shakespeare to become 'Commissar for Public Enlightenment' – or Minister of Information – in the *Zentralrat*.

None of these governments, however, did very much for us, the people of Munich. Most factories were closed. There was nothing in the shops. Our weekly meat ration had reached its all-time low of 250 grammes – half a pound. April-fool-day played a particularly nasty practical joke on us: we woke to see the town covered by a foot-and-a-half of snow, and there was no coal at all, not even on the black market. The civil authorities had almost stopped functioning; the municipal employees refused to accept the emergency paper money which the City was issuing for want of proper cash.

On Palm Sunday, 1919, I was returning to town from a youth club outing. The tramways had been running again, but they stopped half a mile short of the main railway station, and everybody had to get out. The conductors, asked what was the matter, said either 'I don't know' or 'Don't you know?'. I tramped on. There was the rattattat of machine-gun fire to which we were quite used – there had been a lot of aimless and, as a rule, harmless shooting during those weeks. But from time to time I also heard the loud, ugly wham of a mine from the direction of the station.

Suddenly, someone shouted right in front of me, 'Attention – firing starts now!' in a kind of official-announcement voice. And sure enough, the rattattat began from uncomfortably close quarters. I dashed into a narrow side street, where Munich's best-known kosher restaurant was. Perhaps I could have a cup of coffee there and wait until the shooting stopped? But I found

14

that the place was closed, and at this moment another official voice shouted from the end of the narrow street that curious warning – addressed to friend or foe? – 'Attention – firing starts now!' And so it did, after a second or two; I had just time to step into a recess in the nearest building and duck. Then a door opened behind me, I heard the tinkling of a piano, and a girl's voice said, 'Come in, quick!' It was the side exit of a cinema, and my rescuer was an usherette. Undeterred by the civil war all around, the film went on, and I saw the last three reels of a thriller with a lot of shooting in it. For free, of course.

Bavaria's 'third revolution' had begun, the most serious of all. It was a revolution in the Russian style. A new leader emerged at the head of the Workers' and Soldiers' Councils, yet another intellectual from the north of Germany, the young and still unknown expressionist poet Ernst Toller. He had fought in the war as a volunteer, and the experience had turned him into a radical Socialist. On April 7 he proclaimed the 'Soviet Republic of Bavaria', appointed a 'government of people's delegates', and declared the *Landtag* dissolved. The Social-Democratic government which had been formed around the middle of March fled to Nuremberg and from there to Bamberg; they did not want to take any chances: the new rulers in Munich meant business. Following the Russian model, they handed out arms to the workers, and recruiting for a 'Red Army' began.

What I had witnessed on Palm Sunday was the battle for the main station which the Republican Guard had tried to wrest from the rebels, but without success. There were 17 dead and 100 wounded. The Red Army occupied the headquarters of the Republican Guard, the Luitpold grammar school. Rudolf Egelhofer, a 23-year-old naval rating, was appointed Commander-in-Chief of the Red Army and military commandant of Munich; he was a determined but simple-minded man and, as it turned out, a brutal one. It was obvious that he and the Schwabing intellectuals and poets wouldn't get on with each other.

Those of us citizens who ventured out of our houses – one had to try and get something to eat, and twice I cycled out into the country to buy food from the farmers – were treated to an ever-changing display of posters. At least once a day someone declared someone else deposed, groups and factions proclaimed each other dissolved as bloody traitors to the revolution; arms were to be distributed or confiscated, councils and committees were formed or liquidated – at least on poster paper, though there must have been a good many arrests. Toller fell out with Leviné and his Spartacists, who wanted a full-scale civil war. Things grew more and more chaotic.

A few days after the battle of the railway station the exiled Bavarian government in Bamberg managed to tell us by poster that an army for the 'liberation' of Munich was on the march. In fact, the government mustered about 35,000 men, mainly regular Bavarian troops, but with an extra contingent of Prussian mercenaries, the so-called 'Baltic Volunteer Corps': desperadoes and veterans, human leftovers from the war, homeless and brutalized. Gustav Noske, a right-wing Social Democrat who had accepted the unpopular post of army minister in the provisional German government in Berlin ('Someone has to play the part of the bloodhound,' he declared), was responsible for the mercenaries' inclusion in the force that was now moving south, towards Munich. There, the Red Army of about 20,000 soldiers and workers marched out to meet the 'White Guards', as they called them after the Russian model. The Red Army was commanded by an unusual kind of general – the poet Ernst Toller.

Battle was joined on April 17 at Dachau, just north of Munich. Thanks to Toller, who after all had much front-line experience, the Red Army won and occupied Dachau. Egelhofer, still C-in-C of the Red Army, demanded that all prisoners should be shot as traitors; Toller refused. However, Dachau had been merely a skirmish with the vanguard of the 'Whites', whose main body was now encircling Munich. The bloodshed which Kurt Eisner had wanted to prevent began.

There was one ghastly incident which, in Bavarian memory, still characterizes Munich's Soviet period. Shortly before the 'liberation', eight members of a cranky racist association, the Thule Society, were arrested as hostages and taken to the Luitpold grammar school, Egelhofer's headquarters. The Thule people were extremely right-wing, dedicated to the purity of the German race, and used the swastika as its emblem – probably the first German group to do so. On April 30, as the 'Whites' were preparing to march into the town, Egelhofer ordered the

16

execution of the eight hostages, plus that of two government soldiers captured at Dachau, in the courtyard of the grammar school.

The next day the 'Whites' began pouring into Munich. The Bavarian contingents behaved quite decently; they were, after all, among fellow-countrymen. But the Baltic mercenaries turned the 'liberation' into a bloody lark. Trigger-happy and cold-blooded, they began to hunt and ferret out 'Spartacists'. All those found with weapons were shot without trial. I saw the porter of our block of flats come out with an armful of rifles to take them to the mercenaries' headquarters before they discovered them in his room. Within a few days, there were about a thousand dead in the town; among them were 21 young Catholic journeymen, shot in their harmless club – they had been mischievously denounced as Spartacists.

Gustav Landauer was found and killed on the spot by the mercenaries. Eugen Leviné was put on trial, condemned to death, and executed. Ernst Toller and Erich Mühsam, too, were tried but got away with prison sentences. Toller got five years; the volume of poems which he wrote behind bars made him famous – he called it the *Swallows Book,* because his verses were inspired by a pair of swallows that had made their nest on the window sill of his cell. After his release he became one of Germany's most successful playwrights. He fled when the Nazis came to power, and took his own life in New York in 1939, shattered by the tragic end of the Spanish Civil War.

Mühsam remained in prison for six years. He returned to his native Berlin. There he was arrested by Hitler's stormtroopers in 1933; a year later, he was murdered in a concentration camp.

'We went to school in those days,' wrote Golo Mann, the historian, Thomas Mann's son. 'We were given our homework, our marks and punishments, as though everything was all right; except that sometimes the school was closed because of "riots" or lack of coal; that sometimes some minister was murdered, and the schoolboys ran into the street and cheered . . .'

We also started on our literary careers in those days. With a couple of friends I published a little newspaper in our grammar school; Golo, too young at ten for any editorial work, sold the

17

copies in the schoolyard during breaks. We tried to avoid any political or otherwise controversial articles, but once we got caught in a dilemma. We ran a competition for short-stories, and among the manuscripts submitted was one by Golo's elder brother Klaus, then twelve years old. Normally, we wouldn't have touched that contribution, expressionist, highly political and critical of our bourgeois society as it was. But Klaus was the great writer's son and we were little snobs, so we gave him the first prize and printed his story, entitled *The Blaspheming Woman.* The scene was a boring tea party in Munich's polite and reactionary society. Inevitably, they talk about the murder of the hostages on the last day of the Bavarian Soviet Republic. One woman, the outsider in the circle, remarks, 'I don't think the Spartacists behaved as abominably as people say. The murder of the hostages, I suspect, was committed merely by a few barbaric soldiers.' Whereupon the party breaks up in general disgust: 'I won't have tea with Spartacists!', 'Shame on that blaspheming woman!'

I suppose it was that story which put an end to our literary efforts, at least for the time being. We were hauled before the school director. He reminded us that according to the disciplinary rules for secondary schools in the Kingdom of Bavaria — still in force in the Republic — pupils were not permitted to publish anything without the consent of the director; and he threatened us with expulsion. So we had to stop our enterprise.

Were we, the coming generation of German citizens, really concerned about the turbulent events of the times, about politics, as teenagers are today? And were we, like them, rebels as a matter of course? We certainly were concerned, but differently: not about the general state of the world, the perils facing mankind, or the 'establishment'. We had been too much involved for that. We had starved, our generation had lost many of their fathers and brothers. The block of flats opposite the one where I lived had been requisitioned as a sanatorium for wounded soldiers; the daily sight of maimed men had a traumatic effect. After that war, peace was what we were most concerned about, and so our political 'cause' was a simple one: to make sure that yesterday's men, the people who wanted revenge for Germany's defeat, would never get the upper hand.

That we had lost the war did not, at first, seem very important

— it was over, and that was what mattered most, especially to us young people and to the working class. There was also an underlying feeling that it had all been inevitable: all those nations which Germany and her allies had turned into enemies had, of course, proved stronger in the end. Our rulers had suffered from delusions of grandeur, including our poor old King Ludwig of Bavaria with his silly war slogan, 'The more enemies, the greater honour'. We had been hoodwinked. Perhaps our adversaries weren't as vicious as our war propaganda had painted them. The first English soldiers I saw were the drivers of military lorries with Red Cross food who had come up from Italy across the Alps: friendly young men, well fed and in clean uniforms. I talked to them, I had learnt some English. They had come to bring their defeated opponents something to eat in that winter after the armistice.

Only a few cranks, or so it seemed to us at the time, said and wrote that it was not the might of our enemies around us which had vanquished our splendid army — it had been stabbed in the back by the revolutionaries, the traitors, the Jews, the Bolsheviks (or even the Freemasons) in our midst. Events in Bavaria had shown who they were and how they worked, and they were also active in other parts of Germany — in the Ruhr, in Saxony, in Berlin.

We did not recognize the ominous signs, the danger of the 'stab-in-the-back' legend. A new, determined, Socialist German government would soon emerge in Berlin, we reckoned, and then those reactionary cranks would disappear like all the other representatives of the old order, the princes and their courtiers, the generals and the arms manufacturers, the Junkers and the whole caste of Prussian officers and chauvinist statesmen who had led the country into war and defeat.

Prussia! The word alone made Bavarian hackles rise. It was an old antagonism, hardened in many wars and rivalries and resentment before Germany's unification, but reduced to a music-hall joke so long as the going was good in the Kaiser's prosperous Empire. Now, after four years of sacrifices and misery, Bavarians felt again that it had been a mistake to team up with Prussia; Bismarck had steamrollered them into accepting its supremacy, under a Prussian king as German emperor, a prince from that minor upstart dynasty, the Hohenzollern. The

Wittelsbachs, on the other hand, were an 800-year-old family, genuine Bavarians who shared their people's national character, way of thinking, and broad homely speech. A pity that the last of the Wittelsbach kings, that old dodderer, had to go in the November revolution; but he had a son who wasn't too bad, Crown Prince Rupprecht, whom many would have liked to see as king of an independent Bavaria. Besides, he was the last of the Stuart pretenders – there had always been a certain affinity between the Scots and the Bavarians.

Some members of the Wittelsbach family went on living, republic or no republic, in their town house, a few minutes' walk from our block of flats. One of the elderly princes was a frequent passenger on the tramcars which took me to school; he would stand on the open rear platform of the trailer, nodding with a smile when we recognized and greeted him, and he always gave the conductor an extra five pfennig for the ten-pfennig ticket.

The Bavarian separatist feelings petered out. There was one overriding factor which kept the country chained to the rest of Germany – the lost war, for which we would all have to pay. In January, 1919, the Allied plenipotentiaries assembled at Versailles to draw up the conditions of peace for Germany and Austria. A few months later, as the terms of the peace treaty became known, it dawned on us what it meant to have lost a war against two dozen nations. The terms were harsh and humiliating; the bill of reparations, to be paid by a Germany reduced in size and shorn of its former economic power, was shattering. To be sure, much of the cutting edge of the terms was later whittled down; but in 1919, the shock of Versailles, the indignation it created, kept Germany's reactionary forces alive, and the 'cranks' with their stab-in-the-back story and their search for scapegoats found an increasing number of followers.

In the bookshops we saw their literature displayed, most of it violently antisemitic – German nationalism and antisemitism had gone together for at least a century. It was then that I saw, for the first time, books about the 'Protocols of the Elders of Zion', that infamous literary forgery which was soon to play a major part in Nazi propaganda as it claimed to prove a Jewish conspiracy for achieving world domination. New organizations and little parties were springing up and breathing vengeance;

chauvinism and militarism were stirred to a new upsurge.

What German would dare to sign the Treaty of Versailles?

Yet signed it was, on June 28, 1919; and the men who signed it did so in the name of the German people, with the backing of a majority vote in the new German parliament.

In January, 1919, the German people – including, for the first time, women – had elected a provisional parliament, the National Assembly. The Social Democrats got most of the votes; together with the Independents, the (mainly Catholic) *Zentrum,* and the Liberals, they had three-quarters of the seats. Sessions began early in February; not in the capital Berlin, but in Weimar.

The reasons for not meeting in Berlin were stronger than those for picking that sleepy little town in a former miniature principality of Thuringia, right in the middle of Germany. Berlin was, in that winter after the armistice, in a constant state of unrest, though this never reached the stage of a Soviet Republic as in Bavaria. Hordes of soldiers in various phases of demobilization roamed the city. There was a Spartacist putsch attempt, which was defeated in January; its leader, Karl Liebknecht, son of a famous nineteenth-century Socialist, and Rosa Luxemburg, a Polish-born, gentle intellectual revolutionary, were seized by a group of right-wing ex-officers, and brutally beaten to death with rifle butts. Liebknecht's body was found in the street, and Rosa Luxemburg's was fished out from Berlin's main canal. Sporadic fighting went on, and there was always the possibility of a new rising.

Weimar was a name that inspired quiet pride rather than patriotic enthusiasm. Here, Goethe and Schiller, Herder and Wieland had lived and worked at a time when the Germans were really a nation of poets and philosophers, from the *Sturm und Drang* to the romantic period in literature. The town had its own, splendid grand-ducal court, with Goethe, the Privy Councillor, as its main attraction. Both Schiller and Goethe are buried in Weimar, and so is Lucas Cranach. Here Johann Sebastian Bach had been court organist for nine years, and Franz Liszt later spent a dozen years working at Weimar's state theatre.

If the intention was to select a culturally eminent but politically non-controversial place for the National Assembly, the choice could not have been happier. It was also a calm place some distance from the restless industrial areas, and the legislators could concentrate on their work without fear of interruption.

First they elected Friedrich Ebert Reichs President – a rather unexciting, worthy Social Democrat, the son of a tailor from Heidelberg, who had himself worked as a saddlemaker in his youth. On the first day of the November revolution he had been appointed Reichs Chancellor, and tried to save the monarchy, but his party friends did not hold that against him: he was the typical committee man, by nature a mediator and opponent of all violent change.

Then the National Assembly embarked on its main task, that of framing Germany's new republican constitution. Much preparatory work had already been done, since September, 1918, by Dr Hugo Preuss, a leading professor of constitutional law from Berlin. His draft was solid, progressive, reasonable, democratic. Germany was to remain what it had been under its princes, a federal state consisting of a number of *Länder* with their own governments and parliaments, with central Reichs government and *Reichstag* (parliament) in Berlin. The small principalities, of course, had to disappear, as their princes had already done.

Preuss, recognizing the widespread resentment against Prussia, had wanted to do away with the *Land* altogether; its image was tainted, particularly in South German minds, as that of a state of aggressive kings, of authoritarian bureaucracy, of Junkers and officers. But after a good deal of debating, Prussia was allowed to remain Prussia. Otherwise, the Professor's design prevailed: with the voting age of 20 for men and women, equality before the law, freedom of speech and assembly, and strong safeguards against the restriction of civil liberty.

'The Weimar constitution presupposed that Germans were agreed on the basic principles by which they wanted to live together,' wrote Golo Mann. 'The nation had to be reasonably at peace with itself and with the outside world. Were it not, then no constitution could help it. . . . The old authoritarian state was dead and gone. . . . From now on, the people themselves were to be their own authority, there was no other.'

The discussions on the constitution had to be interrupted in Weimar because there was the urgent matter of the Versailles

Treaty. Its conditions were accepted on May 22; they had to be accepted, Germany had no alternative. It was that unavoidable step which, more that anything else done at Weimar, linked that name with the act of surrender in the German mind. In vain the men of the National Assembly tried to inspire something like a new patriotism, hoping that the people would be prepared to see their situation soberly and realistically; but the people did nothing of the sort. The name of Weimar grew almost synonymous with weakness, deception, degradation – the right-wing press (and most of the big newspapers were still right-wing) saw to that. They made the name of Weimar stink, and ever after the nationalists used it to blame the men who accepted the Treaty for almost everything that went wrong in Germany. Few people realized that the refusal to accept it would probably have meant the occupation of all Germany by the Allies.

So we heard little about the work on the constitution, which continued and was completed after the signing of the Versailles Treaty. Yet it was a good constitution, owing much to the experiences of the older western democracies. It could have lasted a long, long time. On July 31, 1919, the National Assembly accepted it. On August 11, Ebert signed it. That day was to be an annual public holiday in the new German Republic.

For us boys, the Weimar constitution had, right from the start, a slight blemish: that public holiday, which ought to have given us an extra school-free day, fell during our summer vacation. That was a special reason for thinking about the constitution less kindly that we should have done.

2
THE GENERALS REMAINED

An old cigar box, my grandfather's pocket lens, various parts from my meccano set, and a camera tripod were the components of a mock ciné camera which I built in the summer of 1919. I took it out into the streets of Munich, pretended to focus the lens on some scene, and cranked away with the meccano handle. There was, of course, no film inside, only a little piece of cardboard activated by a miniature cog-wheel so that it made a whirring noise. Passers-by stopped and stared, children gathered around and admired the 'cameraman' with his cloth cap worn back to front in the genuine film-man's fashion of the day.

That public attention was all I wanted. It was a rather immature pastime for a boy of fifteen, but I was just burning to do something, anything, about the cinema. I was film-mad, and so were many of my friends. Our madness was aggravated, almost unbearably, by the cinema laws: no youth under 18 was allowed into a cinema, except for special 'youth performances' of boring nature films and patriotic historical *kitsch* pieces.

Yet we got around those police regulations; a legal genius amongst us found a nice loophole. We revived our school newspaper, got a friend's cousin somewhere in the provinces, who was over age, to lend us his name as 'responsible editor' (he never saw the paper), and organized 'closed youth performances' for our readers in a suburban cinema. Its owner rented it to us on Sunday mornings at cut-price rates, provided we included in our programmes a stage show: his little daughter dancing. She did it awkwardly and wildly, but he loved her, and dancing before an audience was her greatest desire.

We haggled with the distributors and got some of the latest productions, amongst them – that was our proudest achieve-

Expressionism in the German cinema: a scene from *The Cabinet of Dr Caligari* (1919)

ment — a film everybody was raving about, *The Cabinet of Dr Caligari*. It had been hardly noticed at its first showing in the early spring of 1919, probably because those days had been too unruly; now, in the quieter autumn, the film was put on again and caused a sensation. For the first time, a team of true artists, three painters and an architect, had created a work of powerful emotional impact, fantastic, nightmarish, macabre, in the expressionist style and mood which were the visual language of the period. It was a story seen through the eyes of a madman, set in a world of mask-like faces, threatening shadows, distorted angles. *Caligari* impressed us deeply, as it did the small groups of film-lovers and film-makers everywhere: it was the starting-point of a new approach to the art of the screen, in whose existence and possibilities few people believed.

Later we showed our friends the first large-scale creation of a young director, Ernst Lubitsch, which began yet another new trend in film-making: *Madame Dubarry*, no longer historical *kitsch,* but a successful attempt at bringing people and events of

25

the past nearer to modern understanding; Lubitsch's next subject was Anne Boleyn. The young German film industry had made a good start. In Berlin, the UFA studios, just two years old, attracted talent from all over Central Europe, including Fritz Lang from Vienna; and just outside Munich, at Geiselgasteig in the Isar valley, a new studio complex was taking shape, which excited us boys very much. It was there that an English director, Alfred Hitchcock, shot two of his first films; Michael Balcon came later. In those 'silent' days, film-making was a truly international trade.

As was to be expected, the law was eventually catching up with our film shows. One Sunday morning I alighted from the tramcar and found myself in the middle of a crowd of schoolboys and girls, arguing with a stern policeman in uniform. The cinema doors remained closed: someone at police headquarters had found a plug for our loophole.

Sad as we were, there were consolations. The cinema was only one of many facets of what we felt to be a new era, a radical break with the past that had ended in a tragic lost war. There were outward symptoms of change: our mother's skirts were getting shorter, our fathers' stand-up collars were on the way out; new houses that were being built looked much simpler than the pre-1914 ones, no longer made for showing off but for living in; no more giant sideboards and frilly *art-nouveau* lamps in the furniture shops, but straight-lined, more modest, more practical equipment. Those were the beginnings of a new generation's new style of life, eventually to pervade many spheres, from the visual arts to literature, from the stage to people's private lives. It got the name *Neue Sachlichkeit*, 'new realism', and it replaced the short-lived expressionist style.

We youngsters were, of course, fascinated by everything that seemed to contradict the life style of our parents, of the dead Wilhelminian establishment. We sided with the innovators. For a while, expressionism was for us the emotional manifestation of that welcome upheaval. Munich was the cradle of expressionism; here it had started, a few years before the war, with the movement of the 'Blue Rider' group of artists – Kandinsky, Klee, Kubin, Marc, and Macke. Now the writers had their own expressionist period. Franz Werfel from Prague, I think, was the first novelist and Georg Kaiser from Magdeburg the first

'Long live the Republic' — a political postcard of 1918: the Kaiser flees to Holland while the spectre of Bolshevism is looming

Es lebe die Republik

EXPRESS nach Holland

gez. Rolf Adolf Gärtner München 1918

playwright to shock our bourgeois society with their expressionist literary outcries.

Still, we were also proud of our well-established resident writers. We walked almost on tiptoe past the elegant villa on the Isar where Thomas Mann lived with his children. His older brother Heinrich had, after spending his young years in France and Italy, settled in Schwabing among Munich's *bohème*; a caustic critic of German life under the Kaiser, he had now the satisfaction of getting his most controversial novels published at last — they had been suppressed by the censor. We loved *Der Untertan*, his acid portrait of a typical Wilhelminian creature, and even more his *Professor Unrat*, the story of the downfall of a school tyrant in the clutches of a *femme fatale* (much later world-

27

Karl
Valentin

famous as a film under the title *The Blue Angel*, the name of the nightspot where the Professor's tragedy begins).

The Bavarians are probably the German tribe with the most natural sense of humour. It had been damped and muted during the war, but now it revived to full force again: in the theatres, the satirical journals like *Simplicissimus* and *Jugend*, in the cabarets of Schwabing, in the beer cellars where the working class had their rustic fun. There was, above all, Karl Valentin. No other 'funny man', with the exception of Chaplin, has been the subject of so many essays written about him, all trying to explain and analyse his unique kind of humour. In Valentin it was tinged with tragedy, even madness; it was probably that mixture of the comic and the insane, and especially his absurd and irrational way of thinking and behaving, which endeared him to the people of Munich, equally to the old and to us young.

He was a tall, lean man with a stoop, a pinched and pale face, a long pointed nose, a wide, thin-lipped mouth and sad eyes. In his dramatic sketches he fought a running battle with the material objects of life, particularly with musical instruments (he played several of them). He had teamed up with a tubby, friendly, warm-hearted Munich girl, Liesl Karlstadt, as his partner. In some of their most famous playlets she was the bearded, bespectacled, frustrated conductor of a little orchestra which Valentin, as one of the musicians, kept reducing to utter chaos. Like most great clowns he was really a pathetic figure; afflicted by all kinds of real and imaginary pains and illnesses, suffering from fear of death and persecution mania, and prone to strong phobias such as dread of travelling, he merely extended his private problems to the stage, sharpening his private conflicts into general human ones. As we watched him struggling with things and words, making a mess of everything and upsetting our accustomed logic of thinking, we recognized ourselves, only more so. If our modern Theatre of the Absurd were trying to trace its pioneers: he was one of them.

He set up a tiny show booth at the *Oktoberfest*, Munich's traditional big autumn festival, as soon as it started again after the interruption of the war years. He played the bassoon, Liesl

Germany's Unholy Trinity – militarism, reactionary industry, antisemitic students. Cartoon by Walter Trier (1921)

conducted, but the clarinetist, in a cloth cap, was a new-comer, a medical student from Augsburg by the name of Bertolt Brecht. It seems that Brecht, apart from wanting to earn a bit of pocket money, had been drawn to Valentin because the techniques and mechanics of show business, as distinct from the traditional theatre of bourgeois society, interested him very much. Valentin was a showman after his own heart; for Brecht, who had started out as a near-expressionist poet, was on his way to becoming a playwright, but of a kind different from most German authors of the conventional theatre. He was dead against the German theatrical tradition, rigidly adhered to throughout the nineteenth century: that only comedies should be funny and that any joke was taboo in a drama, let alone a tragedy. He was on the side of Shakespeare who had his clowns in even the most serious plays because he believed that the theatre must provide, in the first place, entertainment. Hence Brecht's interest in Valentin, whom he admired as a natural genius with an unerring sense of eccentric humour and timing.

The play which Brecht had in his pocket when he visited Lion Feuchtwanger, already an established novelist and dramatist, in Munich in 1919 clearly showed these trends. The 21-year-old student — or rather ex-student, for he had by now given up medicine — was 'thin, badly shaved, and unkempt', as Feuchtwanger described him. The play was entitled *Spartacus*, the story of a soldier returning from the war, who is drawn into the Spartacist troubles but renounces the revolution: 'You want my flesh to rot in the gutter,' he tells the revolutionaries, 'so that your idea can go to heaven. Are you all drunk?' A most serious topical theme, to be sure, yet Brecht had shaped it as a comedy. No theatre wanted it at the time. It was performed only three years later, under the title *Drums in the Night*, at the Munich playhouse where Brecht had meanwhile been engaged as a literary director, or *Dramaturg* as it is called in Germany. It was his first success as a playwright.

It must have been at the *Simplicissimus*, Schwabing's most famous cabaret/café which shared its name with the leading satirical journal, where I saw Brecht for the first time. Kati Kobus, the owner, allowed anyone who was not hopelessly drunk or mad to climb on the miniature podium and perform. A good many poets and playwrights, actors and cabaretists who made their way to fame and success in later years started here under Kati's patronage.

Brecht had brought his guitar along, which he strummed amateurishly, accompanying his *Choral of the Great Baal*. It was a somewhat expressionist ballade telling the story of an anti-social poet, a determined 'drop-out' as we would now call him. It was, in fact, the introduction for his play *Baal* which then, like his *Spartacus*, had not yet been accepted by a theatre. He also sang his *Legend of the Dead Soldier*, weird and bitter, with flashes of acid humour. At the *Simplicissimus* one was used to such violent poetic outbursts, but when he performed these two songs a few months later at a cabaret in Berlin there was an uproar, the audience jeered and protested. Much the same happened when the play *Baal* had at last its first night at a theatre in Leipzig. Audiences were much kinder to *Edward II*, an adaptation of the Marlowe play which Brecht had written in co-operation with Feuchtwanger.

I was not sure what to make of the pamphlet-type newspaper which came my way, I forget how, and which I kept for curiosity's sake because it had the crazy title, *Jedermann sein eigener Fussball,* 'Everybody their own Football'. An equally odd picture, of a man with a football as his body, illustrated the title. It was the first German 'organ' of the dadaist movement which had started in Zurich in 1916 as a desperate outburst of artists and writers against the madness of war and was now turning against all traditional notions, against established society and bourgeois logic, mocking new art forms such as expressionism and cubism at the same time. If this anarchistic movement led anywhere at all it led to surrealism, but its protagonists' names were soon well known in the world of unconventional art: Kurt Schwitters, the painter and poet; George Grosz, the political cartoonist; John Heartfield, the inventor of 'photomontage' as a new medium of political propaganda. That football man was, in fact, one of his first photomontages. He had changed his German name, Herzfeld, in Berlin by deed-poll into its English equivalent during the war as a protest against the chauvinistic slogan, *Gott strafe England,* of the Kaiser's propaganda machine.

There were so many beginnings in that first year of peace that we young people were convinced that we were witnessing a

31

wonderful burial of all that had been rotten, reactionary, stuffy, unhealthy in Germany. Oh, yes, and there was jazz – it came from the New World, a revolutionary kind of music for dancing, together with a new kind of dance, the foxtrot. Our musicians didn't quite know what to do with it, except that they now called themselves 'jazzbands' and had to learn to play obscure instruments such as the banjo and the saxophone. As an amateur pianist I tried to master a piece which, misguidedly, was then considered the very essence of jazz – a novelty number called *Kitten on the Keys*. Only when the first English jazzband came to Munich on its Continental Tour early in 1920 did we get a whiff of the genuine article. They were all girls, and I fell passionately in love with all six of them.

We were paying little attention – too little, as it turned out – to a libel action that was going on at a Berlin high court in the winter of 1919–20. The two central characters were Karl Helfferich, a

32

right-wing politician and former Minister of Finance under the Kaiser, and his republican successor, Matthias Erzberger, a member of the Catholic *Zentrum* Party in the *Reichstag* since 1903. Erzberger had become one of the politicians most hated by the nationalist Right which identified him with the legendary 'stab-in-the-back' of the glorious and victorious German army in 1918.

There was a curious story about how that poisonous legend had originated, or at least how the term which 'explained' Germany's defeat had been coined. Erich Ludendorff, Field Marshal Hindenburg's right-hand man in the war, had fled to Sweden (disguised and with blue-tinted glasses, we were told) when the German army was on the run. Early in 1919 he returned, and was soon invited to dinner by the head of the British Military Mission in Berlin, General Sir Neill Malcolm. It was like a friendly get-together of the opposing team leaders after a cricket match. Ludendorff, however, used this social occasion to launch a tirade against the 'traitors' who, just when his army was about to win the war, had started a revolution behind the front.

'Do you mean to say,' asked Sir Neill, 'that you were stabbed in the back?'

'Yes, yes,' Ludendorff nodded eagerly, 'we were stabbed in the back.' The scapegoat for Germany's defeat had been discovered; the stab-in-the-back became the watchword among the German officer class and all who had believed in the military prowess of the fatherland: after all, no less an authority than a British general had said that the surrender was forced on the army by the traitors at home.

One of them had been in that railway carriage in the forest of Compiègne to sign the Armistice on Germany's behalf – Erzberger. A stolid, honest, peace-loving Roman Catholic from Swabia, he had already in 1917 incurred the wrath of the militarists by moving a 'Peace Resolution' in the *Reichstag,* demanding immediate negotiations with the Allies; it was passed with the votes of the Social Democrats and other moderate parties and could have ended the war a year earlier, but the military blocked it. In 1918, Erzberger accepted the thankless post of Secretary of State and regarded it as his patriotic and humane duty to negotiate and sign the Armistice to end the war. Ever since, he had been branded as the principal *Novemberver-brecher,* 'November criminal', by the Right.

In 1919, when Erzberger was appointed Minister of Finance in the new republican government, Helfferich published a savage pamphlet against him under the title 'Away with Erzberger'. It was full of the gravest personal insults, and Erzberger saw himself forced to sue Helfferich. During the trial, a young ex-ensign from an aristocratic family tried to assassinate Erzberger, but the bullet hit him only in the shoulder. A few days later, Erzberger was in court again.

The most prominent witness, called by Helfferich's defence counsel, was Hindenburg. The judges all but stood to attention when he entered the court room. He ignored the lawyers' questions and read out a long prepared statement, all about the stab-in-the-back. He was not called to testify again. As he left the court building, a huge crowd cheered him – there seemed to be crowds of every political hue available in Berlin for cheering or jeering in those days. The government got Hindenburg out of Berlin and back to his country estate as quickly as possible. The stab-in-the-back myth was now firmly established.

The judges – reactionaries all of them – gave Helfferich a nominal fine but accepted the main accusations of the pamphlet against Erzberger as proved. He resigned as Minister of Finance and more or less withdrew from political life, though his constituents in Württemberg re-elected him to the *Reichstag.* The forces of reaction had triumphed over one of the best men Germany had ever had; but they feared that he was only biding his time before making a comeback – he was still in his mid-forties. He had to be silenced for good.

If we had failed to recognize the significance of the trial, the day after its end in March, 1920, woke us up to reality with an unexpected shock. There was rebellion, a putsch; in fact, a double putsch – in Berlin as well as in Munich, though the connection of the two coups remained somewhat obscure. This time, it was not the Spartacists or some other leftist group trying to seize power; it was the reaction, yesterday's men who seemed determined to put an end to the young Weimar Republic.

Few people had ever heard the name of Dr Wolfgang Kapp before he proclaimed himself Reichs Chancellor. He was a senior civil servant from East Prussia, typical of most of the nationalist and monarchist civil-service men whom the timid revolution of 1918 had failed to replace, and who were still in control behind the scenes.

Now Kapp had come out into the open, for some unknown reason chosen as the figurehead of a new government controlled by the old powers; and the choosing had been done by the army, which put a senior officer, General von Lüttwitz, at Kapp's elbow to keep an eye on him. There was a slogan of the Left which we had ignored as mere propaganda, but which now turned out to be the awful truth: 'The Kaiser went – the generals remained.'

What had triggered off the 'Kapp putsch', as it came to be called, was one of the most painful clauses of the Versailles Treaty: the reduction of the German army to a minimum, to a mere 100,000 men, called the *Reichswehr*. The officers and men of the old army who had been, or were to be, sacked – including those whom the peace *Diktat* by the Entente demanded should be tried as war criminals – formed a hotbed of rebellion. German militarism and nationalism, provoked to new heights of fury, would not give in; these reactionaries were determined to chase away the traitors who has signed the Armistice and the Versailles Treaty and were now calling themselves a democratic government.

Kapp and Lüttwitz were supposed to do the job. Their little army, which marched into the government area of Berlin through the Brandenburg Gate, consisted mainly of 'Free Corps' troops, mercenaries and rebellious units whose dissolution the Allies had demanded, so far in vain; prominent among them was the 'Ehrhardt Brigade', ex-marines commanded by a military adventurer, Captain Ehrhardt. On their heels Dr Kapp moved into the Chancellery in the Wilhelmstrasse and issued a proclamation that he was now head of the new Reichs government, with General Lüttwitz as his second-in-command. The statement was given to the press by an information officer they had appointed; it was no other than the notorious imposter Ignatius Timothy Trebitsch Lincoln, a Hungarian Jew who had been, in turn, a Methodist preacher in Canada, an Anglican curate in Kent, and (from 1910) the Liberal Member of Parliament for Darlington. He sat for less than a year. At the outbreak of the 1914 war he seems to have worked as a German spy in London, but was arrested merely on a forgery charge. He made a dramatic escape, was caught again, and convicted and deported from Britain in 1919. He turned up in Germany, where he got in touch with the putsch plotters, persuading them that he could help them to overthrow the republican government, and to establish the best possible relations with Britain. The choice of Trebitsch Lincoln as press chief was symptomatic of the amateurish and confused character of the whole putsch.

What did Kapp and his men want? Everyone of the plotters probably had a different plan, each of them acted of his own accord. Kapp himself was naive enough to want the Kaiser back, Lüttwitz to tear up the *Diktat*. Other putschists indulged in personal revenge, arresting Prussian ministers and any left-wing politicians they could find. Kapp sent a couple of emissaries to the Reichs Bank, demanding ten million marks in cash for his new government; the Reichs Bank managers, being civil servants, stuck to their regulations and refused to pay any money to 'unauthorized persons'. The emissaries turned tail and reported back to Kapp, who resigned himself to heading a penniless government; it never occurred to him to take the money at gun point.

Amidst the confusion of the Kapp putsch, Germany's new-fledged armed force, the *Reichswehr,* kept well out of the way. Its organizer, General von Seeckt − an old-style officer by his background, a republican commissioner according to his official position − ordered the soldiers to stay in their barracks to avoid any conflict. *'Reichswehr* does not shoot at *Reichswehr,'* he declared firmly.

But the Social-Democratic Party did the only sensible thing: it called a General Strike to render the putschists helpless. The trade unions joined in at once; the factories closed down, the trains and tramcars stopped, there were no newspapers, no electric light (at least not in Berlin), and the workers went out into the streets. Spontaneous rallies and demonstrations formed all over the capital, much to the rebels' astonishment, for they had expected the masses to be on their side. They managed to hang on for four days, during which Trebitsch Lincoln embarked on various schemes of his own. He asked one of the putsch supporters, the wealthy wine salesman Joachim von Ribbentrop, to come to his office in the Chancellery to meet two sympathizers from Munich; one was the poet and playwright, alcoholic and drug addict Dietrich Eckart, who had helped to start a new nationalist party, and the other a committee member, a not-yet-demobbed corporal by the name of Adolf Hitler. These two had travelled to Berlin in a Bavarian airforce plane (as the railways had stopped) to make contact with the rebels.

They came too late. It was all over. Kapp, after trying in vain to negotiate with the Reichs government he claimed to have overthrown, declared his 'resignation'. The Ehrhardt Brigade marched out the same way it had come, via the Brandenburg Gate, but this time through a cordon of jeering, fist-shaking Berlin workers. The mercenaries, infuriated, shot into the crowd with machine guns and clubbed a teenager to death with their rifle butts. That was the tragic end of a farcical episode.

Trebitsch Lincoln disappeared, then turned up again in his native Hungary and eventually as a Buddhist monk in Tibet, where he presumably died.

The putsch we had in Munich was of a rather different kind. On the day of Kapp's appearance in Berlin, posters – then the usual form of political announcements – informed us that the Social-Democratic Bavarian government had resigned and a coalition cabinet was taking over, without the Social Democrats (who in fact never returned to power in Bavaria during the whole Weimar period). The new head of government was Gustav von Kahr, a senior civil servant like Kapp, picked and backed by the generals like him. He, too, was a reactionary monarchist, but of the Bavarian brand; he came from an aristocratic family which had served the Wittelsbach kings for generations. Although a Protestant, Kahr was one of the leaders of the Bavarian People's Party, nominally affiliated to the Roman-Catholic *Zentrum* Party in the rest of Germany but with strong separatist leanings – in other words, anti-Prussian. With a man like Kahr in power, Bavaria was just a step from becoming independent, thus breaking up the Republic.

The Bavarian military, now in control, decided to send those two men, Eckart and Hitler, to Berlin as 'liaison officers' with Kapp and company. The army's choice may have seemed absurd – why did they dispatch an NCO to Berlin instead of some general? However, there were certain reasons. After the end of the Munich 'Soviet Republic', Hitler had managed to become one of the undercover agents of the army, with the special job of keeping an eye on some of the innumerable little groups, sects, and miniature parties that were springing up in 1919. One had been founded by the right-wing extremists of the Thule Society (which had lost eight of its members in the 'murder of hostages' during the Soviet troubles); it was called 'German Workers' Party', with the swastika of the Thule Society as its emblem.

Hitler's task for the army was to report on the activities of these parties, infiltrating them as a new member if necessary; the military wanted to know where they had to look for sympathizers and where for opponents – just in case. In the course of these duties, Hitler attended in September, 1919, a meeting of that new 'German Workers' Party' in a back room of the Sternecker beer 'cellar', a large brewery with a garden which I passed every day on my way to school, and where I often went with my family for a sausage supper in the open air. These traditional *Bierkeller* – Munich has always had many of them – are not really cellars but popular establishments for all kinds of purposes so long as these are based on the consumption of beer: for spending a summer evening under the chestnut trees, for mass rallies in the big hall, for masked balls in the carnival season, for party meetings and committee sessions in the back rooms.

Hitler came in civilian clothes as an observer. According to his own report there were 45 people present – shopkeepers, soldiers, students, craftsmen, bank clerks, some teachers, a doctor, a writer, a chemist, a couple of engineers, and one girl, the daughter of a judge. Many were members of the Thule Society, the cradle of the new party, founded to establish a mass basis for the reactionary aims of the Society. One of the speakers on that evening, a professor, called for the separation of Bavaria from the Reich and its union with Austria. This excited Hitler the 'observer', who was after all an Austrian himself, so much that he spoke in the discussion.

It was his first public speech. He argued passionately against the professor's idea of separation; on the contrary, Austria should be included in a greater Germany, making her powerful again. He turned out to be a good speaker, and at the end of the

38

...airman, the toolmaker Anton Drexler,
...political pamphlets into Hitler's hands. A
... was informed by postcard that he had
...t ever having applied) as a new member of
...' Party'. Although it had only 54 members,
...d had, for propaganda reasons, the ex-
...5.

...a of being a member; Drexler's pamphlet,
...on 'un-German internationalism' and the
...sed what he himself had been thinking, and
...ler's 'plan for a new world order based on
...That seems to have been the first time those
...d together in print.

...ning of Hitler's political career. Some time
...of 1919 I read his name in our daily paper. It
... in the report on a speech he made in the
...Munich's best-known beer cellar. There, the
...much larger, and he spoke for half an hour. The
...as the Party's programme points, demands which
...y familiar to us newspaper readers from speeches by
...ical mountebanks: abrogation of the Versailles
...e return of Germany's colonies, the removal of the
...traitors' in the Berlin Reichs government; and all the
...nd other 'people of non-German blood' should lose their
citi... .is' rights.

I don't think we were shocked or alarmed; we had heard it
many times before in that first year of the Republic, for instance
from General Ludendorff, who was now devoting himself to attacks on the sinister, supra-national powers that, according to
him, ruled the world: the Jews, the Catholics, and the
Freemasons. He and his muddle-headed soul-mate Mathilda, an
upper-class virago, appeared to us as no more than a couple of
ridiculous cranks.

For Hitler, the Hofbräuhaus speech – which, said the newspaper, whipped the audience into a frenzy – started the acceleration of his rise in the Party. He was elected to the committee as
its member number 7, with a new membership card. Another
meeting at the Hofbräuhaus, in February, 1920, had to be held
in the large hall: two thousand people came. He was now one of
the leaders of the Party, second only to Dietrich Eckart. The

39

military recognized the movement as a politically important factor; and so Hitler and Eckart were sent to Berlin in a special plane. The Kapp rebels, the military hoped, would help to return Germany into their hands and bring back the monarchy. But the two liaison men had to fly back to Munich empty-handed. A short time later, Hitler was demobbed; now he was free to devote all his time to his Party.

In Munich, Kahr had meanwhile made himself Bavaria's new ruler. This, much more than beer-cellar speeches, alarmed us. Kahr assembled the most reactionary group of men to serve as his ministers – people we had hoped to see never again in government jobs. Would they now take Bavaria out of the Reich, away from the Social-Democratic central government in Berlin?

However, the Kahr men had decided to bide their time, content with sabotaging every law and regulation emanating from Berlin. They were in no hurry; things were going their way anyhow.

We saw Hitler's name more and more often on the posters announcing meetings of the 'German Workers' Party'. In the summer of 1920, the name was changed to 'National Socialist German Workers' Party', NSDAP for short. But the word *Nationalsozialisten* was rather long, and when I heard it first I thought that since the *Sozialisten,* the Social Democrats, had the short nickname *Sozis* in everyday language, the obvious nickname for the new crowd would be *Nazis*. And sure enough, that was what they now began to be called; but I never expected them to accept the name themselves. For 'Nazi', an abbreviation of the christian name Ignatius, was the popular nickname for a feeble-minded country yokel in the Bavarian peasant theatre and in humorous folk stories. Surprisingly, the name caught on even among Hitler's followers.

It was a matter of course that he adopted the *Hakenkreuz,* the swastika, as the Party symbol, taking it over from the Thule Society. Their swastika had curved hooks as it was derived from the ancient sun and life wheel to be found in eastern countries, particularly in India. A Munich dentist redesigned it for Hitler, putting a black, angular swastika in a white circle and surrounding the whole with a red square frame; another Party member, a goldsmith, designed a gold and enamel badge to be worn on members' lapels. The colours of the big swastika banners were black, white, and red – quite intentionally those of the defunct imperial Germany.

New names of Party speakers appeared on the posters. There was Alfred Rosenberg from Reval (now Tallinn) in Estonia, who had studied architecture in Moscow but fancied himself as a philosopher; he was the chief propagator of the 'Protocols of the Elders of Zion' in post-war Germany. His *magnum opus,* entitled *Myth of the Twentieth Century,* was accepted by the Party as its bible, but Hitler himself once confessed that he had been unable to read it through; it was as diffuse and obscure as it was boring. Perhaps this was the main reason why he, despite his limited literacy of which he was aware, decided to produce his own Party bible as soon as he could find the time.

Another new name was that of Rudolf Hess, born in Alexandria, the son of a German export businessman. Some of my older friends who were students at Munich's University knew him well; he had been Hitler's commanding officer in the war for a while, but enrolled as a student in 1919. He organized meetings and demonstrations of right-wing undergraduates. Ex-General Haushofer, the creator of 'geopolitics' as a justification for Germany's plans of territorial conquest, took Hess on as his research assistant. Hess seemed, at least to my friends, slightly weak-headed, always in search of some great cause to which he could devote his life, and Hitler's Party was just what he had been searching for.

Rosenberg, Hess, and Eckart were the kind of 'intellectual élite' by which Hitler wanted to be accepted as an equal. Their Party office was still a back room in the Sternecker cellar—small, dark, bare; the only splash of colour was two swastika flags at the door. New members were now joining in a steady stream, at an annual subscription of one mark (which, in 1920, still bought one or two sausages). By the end of the year, there must have been a thousand paid-up members; six months later, there were three thousand, and twice as many came to one of the first mass meetings outside the beer halls, in the Circus Krone. This was our favourite place of entertainment on the fringe of Munich, but we boys went only when the show consisted of clowns and artistes and animals and not of political speakers.

The money was now rolling in for the NSDAP, and it moved to proper new headquarters nearer the town centre. Old Drexler was pushed out of the way, and Hitler was the boss. But he was no longer content with being called something as dull and bureaucratic as 'chairman'. At a rally in the circus in 1921, he announced to his followers that he had created a new title for himself: *Der Führer,* The Leader.

At the end of June, 1921, Erzberger told the executive of his *Zentrum* Party that he was now prepared to resume his political activities. Two months later he was taking a walk near a holiday resort in the Black Forest. There was a burst of revolver shots which killed him. The assassins were two former officers of the Ehrhardt Brigade. They had false passports in their pockets, which enabled them to escape to Hungary. The Berlin authorities asked for their extradition, but Hungary was now being ruled by the reactionary Admiral Horthy and his clique, and the request was refused. The German police caught only a former naval lieutenant, a Kapp putschist who had helped the murderers to escape; he was acquitted by a provincial German court.

The worst thing about Erzberger's assassination was the shameless joy with which it was greeted by large sections of the German people. We were appalled to hear and read arguments in favour of 'removing' the *Novemberverbrecher,* and the term *Feme* cropped up with alarming frequency. It meant a medieval kind of kangaroo court; people who were charged with some offence against the community but refused to attend a self-constituted citizens' 'court' were outlawed, liable to be killed by anybody who found them. Ten months after Erzberger's assassination, the *Feme* claimed another victim, Walther Rathenau.

He was one of the most outstanding men, but also one of the strangest characters. His father had founded the first, and still largest, electrical company in Central Europe, and Walther was born into the upper stratum of Germany's industrial society. He was a Jew but he hated being one and adored, as we know from his profuse writings, the mythical image of the Germanic superman – the blue-eyed, blond Nordic Siegfried. Not as a confused teenager, but as a leading industrialist of fifty, hooked on the ideas of Nietzsche, Gobineau, Richard Wagner, and Houston Stewart Chamberlain, he wrote things like this:

> Aristocratism was invented by the Germanic race, . . . Nothing is more disgusting than the envy of the slaves, which demands equality. . . . In the northern sagas the artisans are always subterranean, dark, dwarfish, an alien race: proof that the men of courage and light were not active in the arts. . . . The romantic idea of race will glorify the pure northern blood and create new concepts of virtue and vice. . . . The racialist concept will be contested by the desperate ones who fear extinction, until there comes cognition that the free tribes became noble only by shedding fear and desire. . . . The weak one envies the strong one and his strength . . .

Alfred Rosenberg said much the same things in his pseudo-philosophical scribblings.

Yet there was another, completely different side to Walther Rathenau. He was a brilliant and efficient organizer in his huge company, an outstanding administrator and minister. During the war, as the head of the government's economic supply department, he invented the rationing of food and raw materials, thus enabling Germany to hold out against the Allied blockade. He was devoted to the Kaiser but accepted the post of Minister of Reconstruction in the Republic. Early in 1922, he was appointed Foreign Minister, and began to work tirelessly to overcome Germany's post-war isolation and to secure a reduction of her burden of reparations.

In April, 1922, at Rapallo, he met the Soviet Foreign Minister — the first western statesman to do so. The result was a treaty between Germany and Russia for the mutual renunciation of reparations and the resumption of diplomatic and economic relations. This first agreement between the Bolsheviks and a democratic state was branded as a 'pact with the devil' by Germany's nationalist and antisemitic circles, and unleashed a wave of violent hatred against Rathenau.

Around that time I happened to visit a modest Munich restaurant for an evening meal, without knowing that it was the regular haunt of one of the 'uniformed' students' associations.

43

Munich's social and public life was becoming increasingly dominated by these rowdy, reactionary young bullies, mostly from the north and the Rhineland, the sons of big landowners and wealthy industrialists, for poor families were unable to send their offspring to universities in those days. A crowd of undergraduates, in their traditional embroidered jackets and with their sashes and monkey caps, were having their ritual drinking night in a back room; they had left the door open just to annoy us other guests with their bawling, ribald singing. The chorus of one of their songs — repeated so often that every listener got the message — went something like this:

> Bump off Walther Rathenau,
> that goddamed bloody Jewish sow!

Even in the *Reichstag* the hatred of Rathenau was given vent. Helfferich, for the German Nationalist Party, spoke in violent terms against the Foreign Minister. The right-wing press kept hinting that he was one of the three hundred 'Elders of Zion' plotting to rule the world for Judaism. No one in Germany, except some Jewish intellectuals, had taken any notice of the publication, a year earlier, of the discovery by Philip Graves, *The Times* correspondent in Constantinople, he had come by accident upon definite proof that the notorious 'Protocols of the Elders of Zion', by now a bestseller in Germany, were an insidious forgery. Philip Graves (by the way, a half-brother of the poet and novelist Robert Graves) found in Constantinople a copy of a French pamphlet of 1864, entitled 'Dialogue in Hell between Machiavelli and Montesquieu', a sharp satirical attack on the oppressive regime of Napoleon III, written by a Paris lawyer who promptly landed in gaol for it. The text consisted mainly of Machiavelli's counsel on how to usurp and exercise power by all kinds of 'traps and tricks', very much as Louis Napoleon had done it. Graves realized at once that this was exactly the same text as that of the 'Protocols' — only it was not the unscrupulous Italian schemer speaking, but Theodor Herzl, the founder of the Zionist movement, laying down the guidelines for Jewry's conquest of the world before an assembly of Jewish 'Elders'! An eccentric Russian philosopher, prompted by the Tsar's secret police, had committed the crude forgery by substituting international Jewry for the Machiavellian Napoleon III.

In the Weimar Republic of the early 1920s, the insinuation that some prominent Jew was one of those mythical 'Elders' was as good as a threat of assassination. There are some indications that Rathenau not only knew that his life was in great danger, but that he even provoked his own violent death. For instance, he insisted that the police should withdraw the security men who were supposed to guard the Foreign Minister.

On the morning of June 24, 1922, Rathenau drove as usual in his open motor-car from his villa in the outskirts of Berlin towards the Foreign Ministry in the Wilhelmstrasse. A powerful touring-car with two men in the passenger seats followed and overtook him. One of the men riddled Rathenau with bullets from a sub-machine gun, the other threw a hand grenade at him, which ripped his body to pieces. The murderers had done their job to perfection.

They, and the men behind them who had organized the assassination, belonged to various groups of the extreme Right, including the Ehrhardt Brigade; several had taken part in the Kapp putsch. The two killers, an ex-naval officer and an engineer, as well as their driver were blue-eyed, fair-haired young men, exactly the type of Nordic Germans of 'courage and light' whom their victim had admired so much throughout his life. They escaped and hid in the castle of a sympathizing aristocrat. There was some shooting when the police closed in; one of the assassins was killed, the other shot himself. The driver of the touring-car was found and arrested; so were a few of the organizers.

Their trial revealed much of the mental confusion among certain sectors of Germany's youth. The assassins' imagination had been steeped in the myth of the 'Elders of Zion', with Ludendorff and Rosenberg as 'authorities' for the conspiracy of world Jewry against Germany. The murder had been timed to coincide with the summer solstice, which is celebrated in Germany on June 24, the day of St John the Baptist, with bonfires on hilltops, and young Germans gathered at nightfall to celebrate simultaneously the turning of the year and the destruction of the man who had 'symbolized the powers of darkness'.

Still, to the majority of Germans, even those who were still hankering after the good old days of the Kaiser, the assassination of the Foreign Minister came as a profound shock. The judge in the trials of the assassins' helpers expressed that feeling in moving words in his summing-up:

> Behind the murderers and their associates emerges the chief culprit — irresponsible, fanatical antisemitism which condemns the Jew as such, regardless of his personality, with all the calumny of that vulgar libel, the 'Protocols of the Elders of Zion'. It prods confused and immature minds to murder. May the sacrificial death of Walther Rathenau, who well knew what perils he was facing when he took up his office, may the revelations which this trial has brought about the results of unscrupulous incitement serve to purify the infected air of our country, now sinking into mortal sickness and moral barbarism.

Noble words! But how long, we were asking ourselves, would that shock act as a restraining force among the 'confused and immature'? I was spending my last school year in a grammar-school class full of boys from the dissolved royal cadet corps, all from families of the lower aristocracy, rowdies and bullies like the students whom most of them were going to join. The teachers never dared to discipline them. I didn't learn much during those months; my main concern was to avoid being beaten up. Rathenau's murder came near the end of the term, and there was a great victory fête in the classroom. I persuaded my parents not to send me back to school after the holidays, though I should have sat for my matriculation exams in the autumn. I would never have passed them in that atmosphere.

Instead, I entered one of Munich's largest factories, the BMW motor works, as a trainee. At that time, their main products were the 'Viktoria' motor-cycles, and for a start I had to mind the automatic machine that made the carburettor screws. Here the atmosphere was friendly and comradely, although I was an outsider among the factory workers as much as I had been among the young aristocrats. I would have stayed on had I not been so clumsy as to get my finger abrased, nearly to the bone, by a tool grinding-wheel. I left with regrets and joined my father in his boring rag-trade business, which was getting increasingly difficult like most business in Germany. The cause was rising prices, for which development a new, unusual term was gaining ground – 'inflation'.

In 1914, one mark had equalled an English shilling, and a dollar was 4 marks and 20 pfennigs. After the war, the mark began to deteriorate, though very slowly at first. The pace suddenly quickened in 1922. At the end of that year, the dollar rate was already about 8,000 marks, rising to 18,000 soon after the New Year. A bottle of beer cost 60 marks, a pound of potatoes 80, an egg 180, a pound of butter 2,400 marks. Wages and salaries fell hopelessly behind these prices, and our savings were melting away. Everybody was bewildered and frightened, nobody knew what to do about it. Where would it all end?

'If I had appeared on the stage like this, I'm sure the critics would have been more sympathetic.' Cartoon by Hans Boht, 1919

3
INFLATION

Curiously, the early stages of Germany's inflation seemed to us acceptable, even welcome. To be sure, in November 1918, at the end of the lost war, the German mark bought no more than fifty pfennigs had done in 1914. But what could we expect? Food and fuel and everything else was desperately short, and throughout history the price of goods in short supply had gone up. Now that the frontiers were open again, the blockade was lifted and the men returned from the war to their fields and factories, all would be well, we thought.

And so it appeared at first. There was work for all. The shops filled again with the things we had been missing. My most sensational experience of those months was my first banana. Once a friend of the family, who had acquired a motor-car, took us all to some remote holiday resort in the country where, according to a rumour in Munich's business world, the first cream cakes were being served again in a café. And so they were; the full-day excursion, which cost our friend a dozen litres of expensive petrol, had been well worth while.

Then came the shock of the Versailles peace treaty and the gradual realization that much of the new bounty would disappear again or become impossibly costly; the average German citizen would have to forget about luxuries. 'Reparations' to an as yet unspecified amount, compensation for all the immense war damage which Germany had inflicted on the world, would be creamed off her economy in goods and money. The mark bought less and less. That was the time when our new daily ritual began: watching the rate of exchange of the American dollar against the mark on the foreign-currency market. For the next few years, that rate was to rule our lives in an increasingly forceful, pernicious way.

Why did the dollar — after all, the currency of a wartime enemy — assume such an enormous importance as Germany's yardstick of values, even as some kind of magic idol? The prewar 'gold mark' had gone with the gold on which Germany's currency had been based. As obedient citizens we had all responded to the official request to hand over our gold coins and golden trinkets to the government which needed every ounce of the precious metal to pay for war materials and food imported from neutral countries; what we got in exchange were paper marks or war-loan certificates.

Now the paper money was no longer based on any solid values. Some measuring scale had to be adopted. America, which had emerged from the war as the richest nation, provided it: the stable, gold-backed, rock-like dollar. As the inflation gathered momentum, a daily 'index', the dollar-mark rate, was published and displayed by all the banks. It indicated the paper-mark prices we had to pay on that day.

Thus the index became the gauge that controlled our daily lives; there was no other way of determining what the paper marks in our pockets were worth, how much they could buy at home and abroad. As the cost of imported goods went up, shop prices rose for home produce as well, and the workers and employees pressed for higher wages and salaries. We found ourselves caught up in a vicious circle, and the dollar index told us the speed at which we were being hurtled around, inescapably.

At first the rate of inflation had an almost leisurely pace until the middle of 1922. Then the Rathenau murder triggered off a sudden acceleration; obviously, the foreign-currency markets had lost what confidence they had still had in the German situation. The assassination of the Foreign Minister was an international shock not only because of Rathenau's standing but even more because the deed revealed the destructive tendencies in certain sectors of the German people. From that time on, inflation — the word was only now beginning to be used in common language — quickened from day to day. But what had started it in the first place, what was its mechanism?

A friend of mine who attended lectures at the Hamburg School of Economics in the winter of 1922–23 heard its director, one of Germany's most respected economists, tell his

49

students, almost with tears in his eyes: 'The truth is that none of us so-called experts has any idea what actually happens in an inflation.' And none could have predicted what was now to follow.

Our rag-trade firm in Munich was tottering. My father and his brothers who ran it had learnt their trade from its founder, my grandfather, according to conventional nineteenth-century business rules. Inflation perplexed them completely. They were used to buying bales of *Loden* − a coarse, dark-green, hairy woollen cloth − from the mills in Saxony where it was made; in the Munich factory it was cut to traditional patterns and farmed out to a small group of homeworkers, mostly middle-aged women, who sewed the material into capes for the rural and Alpine villagers. The capes served as overcoats in cold, foggy and rainy weather because the cloth soaked up the moisture. Smelly, damp rows of them used to hang for hours near the tiled stoves of the village inns in winter while their owners were emptying their stone mugs of beer.

My father and my uncles had learnt how to calculate the selling prices of the capes from the cost of the cloth and the wages of the homeworkers, adding a modest profit for the firm. Now cost and wages went up considerably between the times of purchase, manufacture, and payment by the customers, usually months later. But it did not occur to these old-fashioned businessmen to base their calculations on the expected future costs; the result was that they were losing more and more money on their wares. I suppose that many, if not most manufacturing firms made the same mistake, at least in slow-in-the-uptake Bavaria. I had never been an asset to the firm, and now even the minute salary I was being paid became a burden for it. So it was arranged that I should go to Berlin as a trainee in one of the bigger, more flexible dress-making companies.

I was just packing my things in January, 1923, when the news came that the French and the Belgians were 'marching into the Ruhr area'. What had happened was that yet another conference between Germany and the Allies about reparations had failed, and that the Berlin government − now a coalition led by the *Zentrum* but without the Social Democrats − had fallen behind with payments and compensation deliveries of goods under the Versailles Treaty. Poincaré, the French Prime Minister, took the initiative in an action which, nominally, was merely meant to back up the supervision of reparations: a few engineering experts were to be sent as 'advisers' to the Ruhr authorities, with small contingents of troops to safeguard the experts against attacks.

In fact, it was quite a little army, some French plus a few Belgian units, which occupied the Ruhr basin, Europe's largest industrial area. Mussolini's Italy, although much of her industry depended on Ruhr coal, participated only marginally, and Britain firmly refused to take part at all; the London government was under the impression that Poincaré, the old fox, was merely using Germany's default as a pretext for annexing the Ruhr. In any case, it was a violation of the Peace Treaty.

I arrived in Berlin amidst a hurricane of fury; never since 1914 had the German public been so united in its emotions. Chancellor Cuno, who had been Director-General of the Hamburg–America shipping line but was no politician, found himself quite helpless in that storm; he let his cabinet colleagues take over, and all he had to do was to sign the decrees they had drawn up. Responding to the enormous pressure from all sides, they declared a total 'passive resistance' against the invaders in the Ruhr – the only kind of resistance a disarmed nation was able to put up.

That passive resistance which, it was hoped, would force the French and Belgians to get out, relied on the co-operation of all sectors of the Ruhr population. Wherever foreign soldiers appeared, German workers downed tools. The trains stopped running, the steelworks and factories emptied, the miners went home, farmers hid their food stocks, many shopkeepers locked up their premises, civil servants shut their offices. Employers co-operated fully. In the entire occupied region, life came to a standstill. The government forbade the provisioning of foreign troops; and it promised full indemnification of all who suffered losses – which meant practically everybody, including, of course, the unemployed workers.

Did the German government know what it was letting itself in for? Did it, for instance, fully realize that Ruhr coal did not keep just the trains in the Rhineland running but in the whole of Germany? Had it done its sums – to how much indemnity the industrialists were entitled, how many unemployed had to be kept alive? Did they expect the severity with which the French would react? Not only did Poincaré refuse to withdraw the French troops, but he sent thousands more to the Ruhr, extended the area of occupation, and ordered the military to beat down every form of resistance, passive or active.

Military tribunals were set up and punished brutally all who disobeyed orders. At the Krupp works in Essen, French troops machine-gunned workers, killing over a dozen; nine directors of the company were given prison sentences of up to twenty years. Unwittingly, the French even created a legend of martyrdom which soon helped to recruit masses of followers to the extreme nationalist movements, including the National Socialists: a shady character called Schlageter was convicted of espionage and sabotage by a French military tribunal and executed; the nationalists claimed that the Social Democrats had betrayed him. It was completely untrue, but the legend persisted.

The passive resistance movement was, of course, financed by the German treasury and the Reichs Bank. A fantastic explosion of banknote-printing began, expanding day by day, the denominations rising higher and higher as the mark tumbled and prices rocketed. At the start of the passive resistance period, one dollar cost 18,000 marks; a month later, 28,000. Now the British banks stepped in, trying to peg the mark and thus to enable Germany to hold out against the French. For a couple of months, the dollar rate actually dropped; but the inflationary momentum was stronger, and in May, 1923, the dollar rate resumed and accelerated its meteoric rise. By July it had reached 350,000 marks. In August it shot up to five million. In September it was one hundred million, and the government was forced to abandon passive resistance in the Ruhr − one of the main reasons being that all the official banknote-printing works were by now unable to produce the grotesque mass of paper money needed. Chancellor Cuno had resigned, and a brave, genuinely patriotic man had taken over: Gustav Stresemann, right-of-centre but thoroughly liberal. He considered it his duty to try at least to lead the country out of the chaos.

But neither the change of government nor the end of passive resistance could stop the inflation. In October the dollar rate reached twenty-five thousand million, in mid-November four million million marks. One pound of potatoes cost 50,000 million marks, one egg 80,000 million, one bottle of beer 150,000 million, one pound of butter six million million, one match 900 million marks.

How on earth did we survive that nightmare? What was our life like in that year of galloping inflation, when money went mad and a whole nation with it? One might call it a vivisectory demonstration of the enormous extent to which human civilization depends on its own ancient invention, money.

I had known Berlin quite well from previous visits, but when I arrived early in 1923 for my training period in the rag trade the atmosphere of the capital had begun to change. The Berliners, who had taken the disappearance of the city's imperial splendour with equanimity and even relief, seemed very nervous and apprehensive. In contrast to the people of Munich with their somewhat southern temperament, the Berliners had always liked hard work and the money it brought in return. Now they were irritated by the incessant price rises, by the devaluation of their wages and earnings, whose causes and dynamics they did not understand. There was something alarming, something hectic about their daily lives, and soon it was to become very much more so.

The first thing I noticed in Berlin was the difficulty of finding a room. As in other European towns, housing had been a grave problem since the end of the war during which no homes had been built. But now Berlin's shortage was sharply increased by the great number of foreigners who were flocking in. One had become accustomed to the impoverished Russian émigrés and Polish refugees who had come west from their turbulent countries; but the kind of foreigners arriving in 1922 and 1923 were people with money, long-term tourists with certain aims in mind, most noticeable among them Americans and Japanese. They were buying up things which, in terms of their own sound currencies, cost them next to nothing: not just valuables to take home as souvenirs but houses, factories, office blocks, even whole streets.

Thus the problem of accommodation was the worst of many others for the young people I knew, especially the students. Absurdly, rents were still pegged by law; but the landladies – mostly middle-class housewives reduced to letting furnished rooms in their outsize pre-war flats – could not afford to stick to legal regulations. If they found tenants paying the rent in some foreign currency, that was the jackpot; mark-paying students had to make do with dingy back rooms. In the provinces, too, things were just as bad for the students, most of whom had to live on their parents' monthly allowances which lost the greater part of their value before they arrived by post. You could recognize many a student by his suit which had been turned, or by his greatcoat – a 'fieldgrey' former uniform coat that had been worn in the trenches by his father or uncle.

Occasionally, a student friend would smuggle me into his *Mensa,* the college canteen, for a cheap meal – often hash made of lights. There were also some restaurants where you could get a cheap dish that looked like proper meat; customers suspected that it was horsemeat, but no one cared to ask. To keep the wolf from the door, students tried to find pupils for private tutoring lessons and to get paid in food – butter, eggs, potatoes. And the craving for cigarettes seemed as overpowering as that for food; prostitutes would oblige for a packet of twenty. It was pitiful to see young and old people ask for one single cigarette at the tobacconist's – it was all they could afford. Once I was sent by my firm to deliver a coat to a suburban customer; he gave me, as a tip, one (admittedly very long) cigarette, which I took gladly.

Bartering became more and more widespread. Professional people, too, including lawyers, accepted food in preference to cash fees. A haircut cost a couple of eggs, and craftsmen such as watchmakers displayed in their shopwindows notices: 'Repairs carried out in exchange for food'. Once I was asked at the box office of our local fleapit cinema if I could bring some coal briquets as the price of two seats. A student I knew told me of a wonderful cash transaction: he had sold his gallery ticket for *Tristan* at the State Opera (a few gratis seats were always given to poor students) for one dollar to an American; he could live on that money quite well for a whole week.

The most dramatic changes in Berlin's outward appearance were the masses of beggars in the streets; the queues of old people outside the soup kitchens that had been set up in the working-class districts; and the street markets that had sprung up all over the town. There were no market stands or booths. Men and women, most of them respectably but shabbily dressed, offered trinkets, knick-knacks, watches, even fountain-pens. The vendors were obviously middle-class people who knew no other way of keeping alive but that of selling whatever they had, especially old-age pensioners who were certainly the worst-off sector of the population. Some were just begging for food or money.

But the hard core of the street markets were the petty black-marketeers. They offered anything portable: foreign banknotes, cocaine, wristwatches, matches, which were often scarce, and of course cigarettes, usually English and American ones smuggled from the occupied Rhineland. As soon as a police shako came in sight, the black-marketeers vanished around the corners.

The buyers were usually better dressed than the sellers—people with heaps of money which would be worthless in a few days. The street markets were one aspect of the general 'flight into real values', the only way of countering inflation. Shops, depart-ment stores, and private people who had something to sell were never short of customers; everything was being bought: fur-niture, antiques, jewellery, perfumes, motor-cars, houses. A stockbroker's son I knew took me to his father's garage and showed me six brand-new motor-cycles; the stockbroker, who could not even ride a bicycle, had bought them from the factory. Pictures and sculptures were favourite 'real values', and some artists did very well in those months. One *kitsch* painter among my acquaintances managed to turn his pictures into another kind of 'real value' – a splendid Mercedes.

Those who already had 'real values' such as houses tried, of course, to hang on to them for as long as possible. But it just wasn't possible beyond the day when there wasn't sufficient food in the larder. My grandfather had had his high-class jewellery business on his premises in the Friedrichstrasse, at the corner of Unter den Linden – one of the best sites in Berlin. He had died during the war, the jewellery shop was sold, but my grandmother still owned the house; we, the grandchildren, would have inherited it. But in the summer of that inflation year my grandmother found herself unable to cope; she was in her mid-eighties, utterly confused by the delirious world around her. So she asked one of her sons to sell the house. He did so for I don't know how many thousands of millions of marks. The old woman decided to keep the money under her mattress and buy food for it as the need arose – with the result that nothing was left except a pile of worthless pieces of paper when she died a few months later. Still, she had not starved during her last days.

Working-class wives had developed a system for getting enough food for their families. You could see them hanging around at the factory gates on pay days, by now at least twice a week; wages were, of course, calculated on the basis of the dollar index, and by the afternoon truckloads full of paper money arrived from the banks – where they no longer counted the notes but stacked them and measured the stacks with rulers. As soon as the factory gates opened and the workers streamed out, pay packets (often in old cigar boxes) in their hands, a kind of relay race began: the wives grabbed the money, rushed to the nearest shops, and bought food before prices went up again.

Salaries always lagged behind, the employees on monthly pay were worse off than workers on weekly. People living on fixed incomes sank into deeper and deeper poverty. Those fortunate enough to have industrial shares managed, at least for a time, to keep body and soul together on the dividends, which were index-tied, or by buying and selling their shares with profit–but you had to be very clever indeed to avoid being caught up in the wave of company bankruptcies in the summer and autumn of 1923.

On weekends, teenagers from the towns went on their bikes out into the country to the farmers, trying to get food, but rarely by buying it – the farmers insisted on 'real values'. So we brought them new and worn clothes, hats, scarves, stockings, cutlery, cigarettes, pipe tobacco, or books with pictures in them – anything but banknotes. We bourgeois families had one special advantage: we usually had domestic servants who came from the countryside. While I was still in Munich I cycled out to the parents of our cook, who gave me butter, eggs, sausages, and hams for the wares I had in my rucksack. Once one of my mother's admirers, who had a flour mill in West Prussia, sent her a crate with a hundred pounds of wheat flour – so we started baking our own white bread, quite a rare delicacy in those days. Less welcome was another gift from the provinces, a hunk of goats' meat, which was tough and had to be cooked and eaten at once before its smell became overpowering.

The different fortunes of the shops reflected the mad distortion of a nation's economy in full colours. You could find one shopkeeper who was doing extremely well next door to another who had become desperately poor: it all depended on what they were selling and how clever, or unscrupulous, they were in getting their wares. For it was not only the farmers who were reluctant to exchange their produce for scraps of paper with astronomical figures printed on them; manufacturers, too, were among those who sold as little as possible to the German wholesalers and shops, though for different reasons: they exported all they could — for foreign currency which they tucked away abroad. Export business was booming, inland sales were rather a nuisance to the manufacturers; and so were ordinary customers, clamouring for goods, to the shopkeepers. In those last months of inflation there was almost a kind of civil war between the two groups.

Queues outside the shops began to grow in the morning, getting hopelessly long until the index figure for the day was published by the banks and displayed in the shop windows; then many people slinked away from the queues, unable to afford the new prices. Bitterness was rife; rightly or wrongly, shopkeepers were often suspected of under-the-counter sales to customers with foreign currencies or other valuables. Sometimes the queues dissolved amidst threats and curses when the shopkeeper hung out the dreaded notice 'Sold Out' and locked up. Occasionally the police had to intervene and disperse the furious crowds.

The bookseller to whom I went in Berlin while I could still afford to buy books told me of the experiences of traders in non-essential goods. Some people with too much paper money acquired whole libraries of volumes, preferably in attractive bindings, as 'real values'; contents didn't matter. Twice a week, and usually too late, the journal of the book trade published an index of new book prices. But other businesses, especially repair shops, which needed raw materials such as metal or leather, were often unable to carry on unless their owners bought the materials at exorbitant prices on the black market. The *Schieber*, or black-market profiteer, who dealt in every scarce commodity, was a figure of national contempt and hatred—yet you went to him without scruples if you were in dire need of something you couldn't get by legal means. He wasn't difficult to find; he was everywhere. He supplied you with tins of food and sacks of coal, with dollars and metal objects, usually stolen – door handles screwed off by petty thieves, fittings from cannibalized trains, lead from church roofs.

I managed to get a week's summer holiday in the country south of Berlin, trying to forget the topsy-turvy world of inflation. But it was impossible to get away from it. Every morning our modest boarding-houses displayed the index-controlled price of the day's meals. The trains, running infrequently because there was no longer any coal from the Ruhr, were incredibly overcrowded, the compartments stripped of everything removable. I saw women and children huddled in the corners of freight wagons.

Back in Berlin, prices were now rocketing from the hundred thousands into millions of marks, and soon into 'milliards', thousands of millions. They were increasing not just once a day after the publication of the index, but all the time. You went into a café and ordered a cup of coffee at the price shown on the blackboard over the service hatch; an hour later, when you asked for the bill, it had gone up by half or even doubled.

How did the authorities and the banks try to cope with the incessant demand for more paper money, for still higher denominations? The head of the Reichs Bank was responsible for the supply, and in August, 1923, he assured the Council of State that he had now made arrangements to issue two-thirds of the total note circulation in a single day. He never again made any statements about the matter; less than three months later, the note issue had to be quadrupled within six days. Another two weeks later, in mid-November, the issued notes would have filled 300 railway wagons of ten tons capacity each.

The fact was that banknote printing and issue had slipped out of the hands of the Reichs Bank which, in theory, had the monopoly. Every printing works in Germany was busy printing money on any kind of paper, and eventually even on cloth, silk, and other fabrics. We called it 'emergency money', and it was issued by all kinds of bodies such as municipalities, industrial companies, the railways, and a multitude of public and private corporations. I cannot tell whether they were all licensed to print money; if such a government licence was needed, it was probably granted in a hurry as the state was now totally unable to cope with the demand. The denominations rose from the 'milliard' to the 'billion', meaning a million millions. Money shops had sprung up which exchanged, for a commission, lower denominations for higher ones. A familiar sight in the streets were handcarts and laundry baskets full of paper money, being pushed or carried to or from the banks. It sometimes happened that thieves stole the baskets but tipped out the money and left it on the spot.

There was a dry joke that spread through Germany: papering one's WC with banknotes. Some people made kites for their kids out of them. The exception was the old, brown-coloured, pre-

At the Reichs Bank: Messengers waiting for the daily supply
of paper money for their banks, to be carried in laundry baskets

war 1,000-mark notes; there was a general rumour that one day they would be exchanged for whatever would be then the equivalent of a thousand gold marks. Needless to say, the believers were disappointed.

There were strikes in some factories as it became increasingly difficult for the workers, even with index-tied wages, to feed their families. However, the doctors' strike in Berlin in the summer of 1923 was completely unexpected. It had never happened before. It was an act of despair. The general practitioners on the panel of the municipal Berlin health service received their salaries with such delays that they felt they just couldn't carry on, and they all struck, refusing to see any patients except in emergencies.

I have always had mixed feelings about this affair because an uncle of mine, himself a doctor, broke his colleagues' strike, acting on behalf of the health service board. He organized 'flying surgeries' in ambulance cars which covered the whole of Berlin. The ambulances were staffed by hastily recruited doctors from the provinces. The strikers had to admit defeat. Naturally, my uncle's name stank in Germany's medical circles after that dubious success of his.

He died twenty years later in the Dachau concentration camp.

Throughout that last period of the inflation it became increasingly clear that we, the middle-class people, would end up on the bottom rung of the social ladder as paupers. We had, patriotically, invested much of our savings in war loans; that money was irretrievably lost — some people even said that the state had no interest in stopping inflation because it wiped out the war-loan debts which the state owed us. 'Mark is mark' was the verdict of some brutally impassive government department, meaning that any revaluation of our investments was out of the question. It also meant that private or business debts would not have to be repaid except in those now worthless banknotes.

The reduction of a whole social class, once the backbone of German society, to poverty was painfully visible. Families were crowded together in a couple of small rooms in their large flats, the rest having been let to tenants. Among my acquaintances in the country were a few writers and other intellectuals who had been living in nice little villas; now they were confined to attics or single rooms in farmhouses without any modern comfort.

What we were witnessing was the swift decay of the middle classes, not just economically but morally. Industrious, law-abiding, thrifty and respectable citizens, now helplessly trapped in the catastrophe, had lost all their confidence in authority, which had been one of the traditional characteristics of the German people. Ignoring the law was no longer 'un-German', it was the only way to survive: the state itself was forcing them into illegal actions. Paying taxes, for instance, had turned into a farce; according to that absurd 'mark is mark' maxim, taxes were paid, but in devalued paper money. We all knew that the government wouldn't go bankrupt by any action or default on our part; if it wanted money, it just printed it.

Wading through the bottomless bog of paper money, people tried to identify the guilty. Inevitably, and not without some justification, the Allies were blamed for having imposed their ruinous Versailles Treaty, the *Diktat,* on vanquished Germany, and especially the French for occupying the Ruhr. But the less logically thinking, embittered multitude tended to believe the right-wing extremists inside and outside the *Reichstag,* who simply blamed the whole Weimar 'system' for Germany's plight – weak democracy instead of strong leadership. No wonder that from now on National Socialism was no longer a party of the riff-raff and outsiders of society: it found its most ardent sup-porters among the middle classes impoverished by inflation.

There was another emotional development which arose and grew in those months of galloping inflation: the animosity against Berlin all over the rest of Germany. Decadence, corrup-tion, incompetence, immorality, vice, became almost identical with the *Wasserkopf* Berlin, the hydrocephalus, in the provin-cial mind; and as Berlin rose to be a great cultural centre in the following years, the provinces hated it even more instead of being proud of it.

But during the inflation there was some truth in that unflatter-ing image of the capital. The changed atmosphere of Berlin which had struck me earlier in 1923 was rapidly deteriorating into hectic hedonism, the devaluation of money was bringing on the dissolution of many values of civilized life, especially among the bourgeoisie. To be sure, it was a phenomenon which affected that class all over Germany, but it found its most tangible and conspicuous expression in Berlin.

Amusement coarsened to an extreme degree, no holds were barred in a general ribaldry, a Witches' Sabbath of humourless lascivity. I was never invited to take part in one of the orgies for which Berlin was becoming famous, but everybody knew they were going on in the posh villas in the Grunewald, the upper middle-class residential suburb. In the West End with its main thoroughfare, the Kurfürstendamm, and in the city centre around the Friedrichstrasse, nude shows, prostitutes' bars, homosexual night spots had been shooting up like mushrooms after the rain. Even for a young man like myself, without any prudish qualms, Berlin's night life during the inflation held few attractions, last and not least because one was bound to be fleeced in all those places. Nor did the street scene appeal to me; tarts and queers paraded *en masse* past the pavement tables, winking at anyone who looked like a tourist with foreign currency. It was a pathetic parade; they were poor creatures, most of them in need of a good meal, and many had the glassy-eyed look of the drug addict.

In the early autumn of 1923 my stay in Berlin on a trainee's salary became impossible, and I returned to Munich; life still seemed slightly easier within a family. Those banks which had so far survived were doing well, and I got a clerk's job in one that had two or three branches in various parts of the town. It was there, during the last weeks of the inflation, that I became a profiteer, a black-market dealer in foreign currencies, though not in a very big way.

We were three friends: one was working in a little film company, the other in an export firm, and I had the job of conveying all kinds of business papers between the bank headquarters and the branches twice daily on my bicycle. I did it conscientiously, but with short digressions, secret of course, to my friends.

At the film company they were always in need of foreign currency; at the export firm they always had some and were willing to sell above the official rate of the day. So on my morning round trip I went first to the former and heard from my friend there what they were prepared to pay, then to the latter to 'order' the required dollars or pounds or francs. On my afternoon round I picked up the foreign money and paid for it in marks, then brought it to my film friend where I got the marks back, plus a commission for myself.

I invested my illicit earnings from those deals at once in shares at my bank, where my colleagues advised me what to buy. Thus, I admit, I profited from the inflation, hoping that in the end I would have made a little fortune. I didn't. It was just enough to treat myself to the purchase of a wristwatch.

Others really did make fortunes out of the inflation. While the state was getting rid of its internal debts, industrialists not only 'repaid' with paper money the loans and investments they had received – they even managed to borrow more money from the banks. The man who did this on a gigantic scale and systematically, building up an enormous international industrial and commercial empire within two or three years, was called Hugo Stinnes.

He labelled himself, with affected modesty, a 'merchant from Mühlheim', a mining town in the Ruhr. He had done well in the prosperous pre-war days, enlarging his inherited coal and transport interests, but his phenomenal ascent began with the inflation. He was a strange fellow, and when he arrived at the Hotel Esplanade in Berlin on his frequent lightning trips to the capital, bystanders wondered whether this was really the legendary richest man in Germany. With his round, balding head – he was now in his fifties – and his short black beard, the ill-fitting clothes on his undersized figure and his shy behaviour, he looked completely miscast for the part. The hotel employees told the reporters stories about his contempt for all the joys of life which were almost *de rigueur* for men at the top.

While inflation was at its worst and poverty at its greatest, Stinnes had amassed no fewer than some 4,500 enterprises, most of them bought up with bank loans: iron, steel, and electrical works, newspapers and hotels, shipping companies and cigarette factories, construction firms and sanatoria. Abroad, all over Europe, in America and East Asia, he owned oil wells and forests, sugar plants and aluminium works, cinemas and tanneries, motor-car and margarine factories, usually acquired by means of complicated financial juggling. It

63

was a mammoth assembly of assets, scooped up without any overall plan or basic aim, by a man apparently possessed by insatiable rapacity and lust for power – including political power, for he got himself elected to the *Reichstag* as an MP for the right-wing German Popular Party. His parliamentary speeches, however, betrayed an incredible naivety in political matters.

When he died, in 1924, his empire dissolved into thin air; his heirs were unable to cope with that unwieldy cluster of properties and had to sell them off at bargain prices. The Stinnes fortune, once said to have been larger than Rockefeller's, had gone. But the other German super-industrialists – the Krupps, the Thyssens, the Klöckners – had been wiser, restricting their expansive urges to certain well-defined spheres. They survived in good shape to play weighty parts in German politics in the years to come, not in the limelight like Stinnes, but behind the scenes.

There is little doubt that these big business circles not only thrived in the inflation but gave it a deliberate, sustained, and decisive impetus. Stinnes himself provided some evidence for this. He had forced his way into top-level politics by 1922, and took part in a number of talks and conferences with Allied statesmen on international trade, reparations, and financial policy. The notes he made, posthumously published, show exactly what went on in the minds of Germany's industrial tycoons. In June, 1922 – in fact, one day before his assassination – Rathenau, the Foreign Minister, took Stinnes to a discussion with the US Ambassador in Berlin. Stinnes wrote:

> I analysed the situation in detail. First I stated the reasons why Germany carried out her policy of inflation. . . . To acquire raw materials and export markets for our production, some capital had to be sacrificed. . . . Dreadful as the ravages of Bolshevism had been in Russia, they would no doubt have been even worse in Germany as a mainly industrial country. . . . I also told the Ambassador that the weapon of inflation would have to be employed in the future as well, regardless of the resulting great losses of capital, because only this would make it possible to provide the people with regular work. . . .

The Americans, however, thought that inflation would

bring an extraordinary loss of national assets. . . . (But) they agreed that lives were worth more than money, and they understood why Germany followed a policy of inflation if this was the only way of saving the life of the nation.

Thus Stinnes, from the grave, admitted that Germany's inflation had been a deliberate policy, fostered and supported by big business, by men who calmly took it upon themselves to destroy private property and whole sectors of the population with it. His explanation, that it was all done in a good cause, namely to save Germany from Bolshevism, sounds rather hollow. That was also the cause for which Hitler was soon to collect money from big business.

Symptomatic of the fact that the inflation did little harm to industry and even encouraged new projects was the event of October 29, 1923: the start of Germany's first daily broadcasting service. The electrical and gramophone industries had joined forces to build a radio transmitter near Berlin and equip a studio in the 'Vox' house near the Postdamer Platz, which belonged to the leading gramophone company. The manufacture of receivers (plus earphones, of course) had begun months earlier.

What the newspapers told us about that studio was not very impressive. An upstairs room had been adapted for the purpose, with some horse blankets and old rugs as acoustic drapery. A large carbon microphone with a telephone horn dominated the scene while the 'orchestra', consisting of a pianist and a cellist, provided the live musical programme; when records were transmitted, the microphone was put on one of the three available chairs close to a gramophone. The transmitting equipment had been set up in an adjoining room on a coarse wooden table with some extra boards nailed on to enlarge it. When the producer-announcer was ready to start the transmission he signalled the engineer next door by knocking on the wall with a hammer.

In those first days of broadcasting, the dollar rate reached two million million marks.

Two weeks later it was all over. The inflation was stopped by means of a gigantic confidence trick in which we all joined and which we accepted eagerly.

Ever since his accession to the post of Reichs Chancellor in August, 1923, Gustav Stresemann had made the stabilization of Germany's currency his top priority; whatever pressures in other directions there may have been on the part of big business, he resisted them. His main helpers were three men of widely different backgrounds and characters. There was Karl Helfferich, the former Minister of Finance under the Kaiser, the right-wing politician who had hounded the 'November criminal' Erzberger, rousing the wild passions that led to his murder in 1921. But Helfferich was without doubt a shrewd financial expert, and Stresemann valued the advice of the man he otherwise detested.

Then there was Dr Rudolf Hilferding, an Austrian-born Jewish Socialist, who had been a paediatrician in Vienna before settling in Berlin, studying sociology and acquiring Prussian nationality. He had made a name for himself by some brilliant essays on financial policy, and Stresemann made him his Finance Minister. He gave Hilferding the urgent job of working out a system of stabilizing the mark, using Helfferich as his adviser.

Helfferich came up first with the idea of introducing a completely new currency, the *Roggenmark,* based not on the value of gold, which Germany no longer had, but on that of rye, which it did have. One new mark should equal a pound of rye, the main produce of Germany's farmers.

Dr Hilferding accepted the general idea that the new currency should be backed, at least in theory, by some tangible value other than gold. But he wanted to go a great deal further. After many discussions it was decided to found a *Rentenbank,* a national bank whose assets should be provided by interest-yielding mortgages imposed on all industrial and agricultural property in the country. The new bank should issue bonds backed by these assets, and the bonds in turn were the backing of the new money to be printed and coined – the *Rentenmark.* However, this currency should only be a temporary one, to be replaced in a few months' time by a new, permanent *Reichsmark.*

66

On October 15, the *Reichstag* passed the act establishing the *Rentenbank,* and the date of the issue of the first *Rentenmark* banknotes was secretly fixed: November 15. A few days before, the third man of the financial trio came to the fore – Dr Hjalmar Schacht, until then head of one of the big German banks, but completely unknown to the general public. He was appointed 'Reichs Currency Commissar', with the task of introducing the *Rentenmark* to the nation.

Ever since, popular legend has hailed Schacht as the financial wizard who stopped the inflation; in fact, he did nothing of the sort, coming rather late on the scene as he did. But he was the front man in the great manoeuvre, and his preposterous outward appearance made an unforgettable impression. His overriding feature was an absurdly high, stiff collar – a godsend for every cartoonist. His pinched eyes were hidden behind an old-fashioned pince-nez, he had a tiny moustache, and he always wore a bowler hat: altogether more the picture of an eccentric than the conventional image of a banker. Soon after introducing the new currency he was appointed director of the Reichs Bank, a post he was to hold for seven years and then again under the Hitler regime.

In his role as the magician who had to make one currency disappear and another one appear in its place, Schacht did the trick extremely well – decisively helped, however, by a most co-operative public. For months we had been reading about plans, conferences, preparations and legislation to stop Germany's plunge into the abyss; but who would still trust the politicians and the financial experts? Would they not have stopped inflation long ago if they knew the secret of how to do it?

To call a sensational surprise what the morning papers told us on November 15, 1923, would be an understatement. We were completely dumbfounded to hear that our salvation had already taken place, and all we had to do was to accept it. The new banknotes were already available at the banks; one *Rentenmark* would be worth one 'billion' – 1,000,000,000,000 – old marks; and the dollar would be pegged at four *Rentenmark* and 20 *Rentenpfennig*, its pre-war value in gold marks.

This was the packet of announcements issued by the Reichs Currency Commissar, Dr Schacht, plus a popular explanation how the new currency was backed; but we didn't read the small print. We desperately wanted to believe in it, to trust it, to be paid in it, to buy with it – and, a most important psychological factor, to reckon again in *pfennig*, one hundred to the mark, as we had done in the old days before the nightmare of inflation.

All the world's money exchanges, too, accepted the new currency; thus the great con trick was a full success. It was a life-saving operation, though the patient had lost a lot of blood. There was to be no compensation whatsoever for people's capital and savings that had gone down the drain, not even for those legendary brown thousand-mark notes.

Later, someone at my bank who had inside information explained to me the clever extra trick which Schacht had played on the foreign-exchange speculators who had been making fortunes by trading in dollars and other foreign currencies. They had made the usual 'forward' deals when the new mark and the 4.2-mark rate for the dollar were introduced. Speculating on the continued fall of the paper mark, they had been buying dollars at prices of up to 10 or 11 million million marks apiece; at the end of November, they had to settle their debts for these deals – but the dollars they had bought were now worth only 4.2 million million old marks. Thus they lost fortunes; yet they could have been spared the calamity if Schacht had leaked a warning a day or two before revaluation instead of keeping it a closely guarded secret. In the end, many a high-living money *Schieber* was left with nothing: not even a wristwatch to show for his pains.

Germany's economy began to breathe again. A working arrangement for the Ruhr was made with the French; in the summer of 1924, the 'Dawes Plan' (named after the American head of the Reparations Commission) limited Germany's liabilities at a tolerable level, and the provisional *Rentenmark* made way for the permanent *Reichsmark*. In 1925, the French marched out of the Ruhr.

4
THE PUTSCH THAT FAILED

There was one day during the last chaotic week of the inflation when it suddenly ceased to be the overriding concern of the people of Munich; when the dollar rate, the food and coal prices were no longer the most important problems. On that day, November 9, 1923, something alarming was happening — though at first we did not know what, and only sensational rumours were spreading through the town.

The morning papers, printed as usual on the previous evening, gave no indication. I had been to the theatre, and on my way home by tram I noticed no signs of anything exceptional. But when I set out in the morning on my way to the bank there were no trams, a sure symptom of unrest, and there were excited groups of people at the stops as always when the tramcars failed to turn up. It was no use asking them what was afoot; everybody told a different story. I walked on towards the town centre.

The shortest way took me down a little hill leading to one of the main bridges across the river Isar. Halfway up that hill stands the enormous Bürgerbräukeller; like most other beer 'cellars' it has a very large hall used for events of all kinds. On that morning, something seemed to be going on inside; policemen, some armed with carbines apart from their usual pistols, swarmed around it, nervously shouting at bystanders to keep moving. A few were busy tearing placards from the walls. I thought the whole thing had something to do with the date — November 9 was the anniversary of the 'stab in the back' of the German army, the revolution of 1918.

Suddenly a crowd of young men in various kinds of uniforms, most of them with steel helmets and all with swastika armlets, burst out of the main doors of the 'cellar' and began to form a marching column, or climbed into open lorries. I was not sure whether they had fire-arms, but many carried sticks. The police watched them but did not interfere. My automatic reaction was to get out of the way. As I crossed the bridge into town, the lorries overtook me, with the men on them singing and shouting. The marching column came behind.

It was nine o'clock when I arrived on the Marienplatz, the central square of the inner town. There was a huge mass of citizens, with a couple of tramcars stuck in their midst. A man stood on an open motor-car, speaking. He was in civilian clothes, but a steel-helmeted soldier with a rifle guarded him. In those days before the introduction of loudspeakers, even a stentorian voice carried only over a small fraction of the audience at a large open-air event. Was it an armistice-day meeting? Or had the inflation come to an end all of a sudden?

Someone in the crowd told me that the speaker was Julius Streicher, a teacher from Franconia, Bavaria's northern province; a year ago, he had joined the Hitler party with a little ultra-nationalist society he had founded. He also put its journal, later to become the pornographic-antisemitic *Stürmer,* at the disposal of the National Socialist movement. Now he was haranguing the Munich people – to what purpose it was impossible to hear.

At my bank the shutters were down. The caretaker told me that the manager – it was a Jewish-owned firm – had decided to close shop and send the staff home. So I walked back, past the many fresh posters I had not yet seen:

Proclamation to the German People!

The Berlin government of the November criminals has today been declared deposed. A new provisional national government has been formed. It consists of General Ludendorff, Adolf Hitler, General von Lossow and Colonel von Seisser . . .

In the distance, machine guns started their rattattatt. I had been right in the middle of a putsch in progress.

What had happened the night before did not emerge for some

time, much of it only months later during the 'Hitler trial'; but those events put quite a new complexion on many developments during that fifth year of the Weimar Republic, developments which we had not even tried to understand properly, wrapped up, as we were, in our worries about the inflation.

One of the keys to that understanding was the question why Hitler, still an Austrian national, had not simply been expelled as an undesirable alien by one of the successive Bavarian governments for which he was a pain in the neck with his seditious speeches, his anti-democratic party, his private army of rowdies. The answer was that he was not unwelcome as a nationalist, a fire-eating opponent of the Social Democrats who were dominant in the Reichs and Prussian governments. Hitler's party had been banned in Prussia in 1922 – all the more reason for not doing so in Bavaria.

But where Bavaria's authorities drew the line was that private army of 'stormtroopers,' the SA, partly equipped with rifles, pistols, or at least daggers. In May, 1923, the SA was forced to capitulate to the police when they paraded on the exercise field of the *Reichswehr,* Germany's new post-war army. Nor did Bavaria like the rapid extension of the Hitler movement to other parts of Germany; Munich was now the controlling centre of an organization which Kahr, Bavaria's strong man-behind-the-scenes, began to see as a danger to his own secret plans.

However, nothing could be done to stop the 'German Day' in Nuremberg early in September, for there the figure-head and guest of honour was General Ludendorff, still revered as a war leader despite his latter-day absurd notions. Most of the right-wing extremist organizations, some as small as they were weird, had sent delegates to Nuremberg, and a 'German Fighting League' (*Kampfbund*) was founded. The SA was its dominant member, and a recruiting office was set up in Munich in a tobacconist's shop next door to the bank where I worked. Three weeks after the Nuremberg event, Hitler was appointed 'political leader' of the *Kampfbund.*

In that last week of September, when banknotes of hundred-million mark denominations were changing hands in the shops, the turmoil in Bavaria led to an unexpected climax. Kahr, who had been Bavarian Prime Minister for a year after the Kapp putsch and had been pulling the strings of politics ever since,

71

was suddenly appointed to a constitutionally non-existent post by a desperate Munich government – the post of 'General State Commissioner', practically a dictator. His first act was to declare for Bavaria a State of Emergency. The Reichs government in Berlin was appalled: was this the beginning of Bavaria's secession from the German Republic?

Kahr did everything to confirm Berlin's fears. He declared the national German laws for the protection of the Republic as no longer valid in Bavaria. He avowed publicly that he was in favour of bringing the monarchy back. He broke off relations with Saxony, where the Communists had joined the *Land* government. He took political opponents into 'protective custody.' He expelled over two dozen Jewish families – refugees from Eastern Europe – from Bavaria. Yet he acted with equal determination against the Nazis: no fewer than fourteen of their mass rallies were banned. It became increasingly clear that Kahr's major enemy was Hitler.

Thus there were in Bavaria two opposing forces, both bent on the destruction of the Weimar Republic, both preparing right-wing revolutions. Exactly what Kahr intended to do, and how he planned to do it, was still obscure in that autumn of 1923, but it must have been the separation of Bavaria from the German Republic, dominated, as it was, by Prussia. Then the restoration of the Wittelsbach monarchy would probably follow. Hitler, on the other hand, made it clear that he wanted nothing less than dictatorial power in a new, strictly authoritarian, tightly centralised Germany. He believed that he could pull off a 'march on Berlin' just as successfully as Mussolini had his march on Rome the year before. Kahr as well as Hitler saw their chances of success right now, banking on the support of the great mass of the people in their desperate plight, who were fervently hoping for some kind of miracle that would end the chaos of inflation.

In October, the intensity of the usual quibbles between the Bavarian and the Reichs governments grew until Kahr demanded, in as many words, the resignation of the latter. Expecting some kind of invasion from the north, he ordered units of the Bavarian *Reichswehr* – whom he had made to swear a new oath of allegiance to Bavaria – to man the borders with Thuringia. Kahr's separatist revolution was thus already under way less than two weeks before the fateful November 9. For Hitler, this must have been a powerful incentive to quick action. He had to steal a march on Kahr, blotting out Kahr's revolution with his own.

However, despite all the noise he made with his party and his stormtroopers, Hitler's active followers in the whole of Bavaria numbered only a few thousand, though there were many more party members. A look at their occupations and social backgrounds shows that they were predominantly middle-class, paying their subscriptions regularly, but unlikely to mount the barricades − except perhaps the students. There were teachers, clerks, engineers, doctors, businessmen, housewives; the numbers of manual workers and civil servants were small. Hitler needed more activists in Munich and issued secret orders to his party secretaries in the small towns and villages to send their brawniest members to the capital early in November. It was a curious and slightly ridiculous sight when little columns of burly peasants and cowherds in their traditional costumes − short leather pants, green hats with woodcock feathers, embroidered braces − marched through the shopping streets of Munich as though they were going to the annual October Festival.

Hitler's trump card was Ludendorff. The old general had made his home near Munich, nursing his resentment against the Berlin government that showed no intentions of using his services again, fulminating at the stab-in-the-back that had, as he asserted, robbed him of victory, publishing together with his consort Mathilda pamphlets and little journals about the world conspiracies of the Jews, the Catholics, and the Freemasons against Germany, and sermonizing in favour of a return to the ancient Nordic gods and creeds. Yet his standing among the senior officers, especially those who had been pensioned off, and among the right-wing bourgeoisie was still high. He was convinced that one day he would be called upon to lead a new Reich, or at least a new army, larger than the paltry 100,000 men permitted by the Versailles Treaty.

Kahr ignored him and warned the Bavarian officers not to associate with him. But the *Kampfbund* rally at Nuremberg assured Ludendorff that he was wanted. He was ready, therefore, to march with Hitler, using him as his pacemaker.

73

While I was enjoying a comedy at the theatre on the night of November 8, the Bürgerbräukeller saw what was probably the most farcical attempt at revolution in German history. The large hall had been hired by General State Commissioner Kahr for a speech on his political ideas before an assembly of delegates from nationalist organizations, who had been invited, and any Munich citizens who cared to hear Bavaria's strong man speak. He probably wanted to sound the mood of his potential allies and of the population at large before making the final break with Berlin. He was a mediocre speaker, unlikely to inspire an audience to revolutionary action. Still, the hall was filled to the last seat, and many people were standing about in the aisles when proceedings began at half past seven. There must have been at least 3000 people in the hall.

It seemed that the citizens of Munich were expecting some kind of political sensation, though only one group of them could have foreseen what was really going to happen: the Nazi supporters with whom Hitler had seeded the audience. Otherwise there were businessmen, bankers, senior civil servants, newspapermen, prominent personalities from all walks of Bavarian life, and of course members of various right-wing organizations. Ludendorff had been invited but did not show up. The introductory speech was made by a friend of Kahr's, the owner of Munich's most fashionable cigar shop. On the platform sat General von Lossow, commander of the Bavarian contingent of the *Reichswehr,* and Colonel von Seisser, chief of the Bavarian police force.

Kahr started his speech, reading monotonously from his prepared manuscript, and repeating his often-heard recriminations against the Reichs government, his homilies about the dangers of Marxism. He had been speaking for half an hour when there was a disturbance at the entrance. A small troop of armed men, some with submachine-guns, were forcing their way into the crowded hall, led by a short fellow excitedly brandishing a Browning. It was Hitler.

He had been waiting, increasingly nervous, in the vestibule, sipping from his half-litre glass of beer, waiting for the lorries with the SA to arrive. He called one of his group of followers and ordered him to drive out to Ludendorff's home to inform him that the putsch had succeeded (the first of the evening's

74

bluffs and lies), and that Ludendorff was now expected to join him at once at the Bürgerbräu. He would be made commander-in-chief of the German army – rather a cheek on the part of an ex-corporal, giving a general orders and promising him a job, *and* all under false pretences!

A look-out man rushed to Hitler, reporting that the stormtrooper lorries were just arriving. With a ham-actor's gesture, Hitler swept his beer glass aside, took out his Browning, and signalled the group of men around him to follow him into the hall.

These men were a motley crowd. Among them were Hitler's bodyguard, a primitive and brutal butcher's apprentice; his former sergeant in the army; Rudolf Hess, who was to become his second-in-command in the party; 'Putzi' Hanfstaengl, the son of Munich's most famous art publisher, who had studied at Harvard together with F. D. Roosevelt, and who would have felt more comfortable at home playing the piano than handling the pistol that had been pushed into his hand.

The planned dramatic effect of the group's march into the hall was somewhat marred by the difficulty of pushing through the perplexed crowd to the platform. Kahr had stopped speaking, and saw with dismay that a heavy machine-gun was being wheeled into the entrance by uniformed stormtroopers. Some people panicked and tried to leave, but every exit was now guarded, no one was allowed out, and a few who tried were kicked and beaten back.

At last Hitler arrived below the platform, grabbed a chair, mounted it, and fired a pistol shot at the ceiling. There was a sudden silence in the hall. He jumped from the chair and leapt up the steps to the platform. A police major, hand in pocket, tried to bar the way. Hitler put his pistol at the officer's head and shouted, 'Take your hand out of your pocket!' The man obeyed.

Hitler was now in front of the triumvirate Kahr, Lossow, and Seisser. He turned to the audience and declared in a hoarse, ex-cited voice: 'The national revolution has started. The building is guarded by six hundred heavily armed men. The barracks of the *Reichswehr* and police have been occupied. *Reichswehr* and police are now on the march under the swastika banner!'

That was the second bluff; the three men behind him must

75

have known that there was not a word of truth in it, yet they remained silent.

'The Bavarian government and the Reichs government have been dismissed,' Hitler continued. 'A new provisional government is being formed.' Then he turned to the triumvirate and, still brandishing his Browning, ordered them to follow him to an adjoining back room. His henchmen behind them, they marched off without a word of protest. But Lossow whispered to Seisser, and Seisser passed the word on to Kahr as they filed out of the hall: 'Pretend to play his game.'

Some people in the audience watched aghast as this shameful surrender – for this was what it looked like – took place before their eyes. There were shouts of 'What a farce!', 'This isn't South America!', 'Don't be cowards like in 1918 – shoot!' But no one did.

In the small, bleak back room, still reeking of beer and pipe fumes from some afternoon club meeting (Hess had rented it providently), Hitler sat down with his captives. He began by making them offers they could not refuse: they should join the new Reichs government which he had already begun to form with Ludendorff (a new lie). He, Hitler, would be the leader; Ludendorff was to be army chief, Seisser could be head of a national police force, Kahr 'provincial administrator' of Bavaria; Lossow, too, was to join the government, but Hitler seemed to have forgotten in what capacity.

The three listened in silence, anxiously watching the excited man with his pistol and the armed guards barring the way out. Hitler ended with the threat: 'Anyone who refuses to collaborate with me has no right to live. I have four bullets in my gun – three for my collaborators if they abandon me, and the last for myself.' He put the barrel to his temple: 'If I am not victorious by tomorrow, I shall be a dead man.'

Kahr was the first to answer. 'You can have me shot or shoot me yourself,' he said calmly, 'or just lock me up. A life more or less makes no difference.' Seisser: 'But Herr Hitler, you promised me a few days ago that you wouldn't stage a putsch!' Hitler: 'Yes, I promised. But I had to do it, for the good of the fatherland.' He called his bodyguard to get him another glass of beer.

Suddenly he seemed to get rattled as his prisoners did not

declare their enthusiastic allegiance. He jumped up and ran out on to the platform. Here, during the quarter of an hour of his absence, the scene had changed. Hermann Goering, at that time commander of the SA, had arrived, and occupied the deserted speaker's rostrum. He was in full gala uniform, with medals pinned to his chest – awarded to him during the war as a pilot, squadron leader, and eventually commander of Richthofen's famous 'air circus'. He had joined Hitler's party only a year earlier.

Goering appeared just in time to tame the three thousand people in the hall who were getting restless, despite the threatening machine-guns and pistols around them. What, they wanted to know, was happening in that back room? 'Don't worry,' Goering told them. 'No harm will come to Herr von Kahr, to Lossow and Seisser. They are holding preliminary discussions for the formation of a national government which all of you want.'

'You don't need machine-guns and hundreds of armed men for that,' cried someone, and there was a roar of applause.

'Shut up!' Goering snarled arrogantly. 'You've got your beer, haven't you?'

Now Hitler came dashing back. The excitement in the hall, far from abating, heightened. He seemed to have lost. Again he drew his pistol and fired a shot at the ceiling. 'If you don't keep quiet,' he shouted, 'I'll have another machine-gun put in the gallery!' At last there was silence, and he started anew, calmly and without his usual melodramatic gimmicks. What was happening, he said, was in no way directed against Kahr, who would remain in control of Bavaria. But a new Reichs government had to be formed, with Ludendorff, Lossow, Seisser and himself. 'There are these three men in the back room, wrestling with their conscience,' he said, putting on a touch of emotion. 'Can I tell them that all of you will be behind them?'

Ja, ja,' came the thunderous answer. He had succeeded in swinging the mood of the crowd on his side in a matter of minutes – it was a demagogue's masterstroke. 'In a free Germany,' he went on, now with passion, 'there will be a place for an independent Bavaria!' And he ended on his favourite heroic note; here was the man of destiny pleading for the hearts and souls the people: 'This I can tell you, either the German revolution begins tonight, or we shall all be dead by tomorrow morning.'

Meanwhile, Ludendorff had been brought in. Rising to the occasion, he had put on his old uniform of the imperial army. Hitler told him about the three in the back room who needed a little more persuasion, and who could do that better than Ludendorff? The old general obliged. Lossow and Seisser, remembering their gentlemen's agreement to play Hitler's game, declared their willingness to co-operate, and in the end so did Kahr.

They all returned to the platform. Kahr spoke first: he had decided to take over Bavaria's 'regency' as locum tenens for the monarchy. There was another storm of applause. Hitler, with one of his histrionic gestures, shook him by the hand; then he turned to the audience and declared that he was going to be Germany's new political leader, at least until the 'November criminals', now at the top, had been brought to justice.

Next came Ludendorff, revealing his 'surprise' at the whole turn of events. Lossow and Seisser, too, were pressed to speak, but they did so in vague terms, saying something about a 'fight for freedom'. Again Hitler shook all hands in the vicinity. The rally was over, and the audience were allowed to leave, unhindered by the stormtroopers − except some prominent opponents whom Hitler wanted to be held and taken away as hostages. It was Hess who supervised their arrest.

The triumvirate had also been allowed to leave: that was Hitler's cardinal mistake. Flushed with victory, he was now convinced that he was irresistible and infallible, and that his genius would overcome any difficulties that might still arise. But his greatest misconception was that, like all great deceivers and bluffers, he regarded his opponents as too stupid and too honest to play the same tricks on him.

By half past ten, the Bürgerbräu was empty, apart from the Nazi leaders who used it as their putsch headquarters, and an SA unit who guarded them. At the other end of the town, in the Löwenbräu 'cellar', the *Kampfbund* was holding a parallel meeting. Here, about 1,800 members, the majority in uniform, were drinking beer while being entertained by a couple of brass bands, and waiting for news about the putsch. The principal speaker was Major Ernst Röhm, formerly of the *Reichswehr*. At nine o'clock he was called to the telephone and received the coded message, 'Happy event'.

He passed the good news on to the crowd in the hall: the putsch had succeeded. Then he put himself at the head of a column of *Kampfbund* members and marched off with them. A journalist told me later of a somewhat comic scene; as the marchers passed the tram stop they saw the policemen who had watched the meeting, waiting impatiently for the next tramcar to get to their headquarters and report personally about the rebellious activities they had just witnessed. In those days the Munich police was only modestly motorized.

Röhm took his men to various military establishments, first to the undefended *Reichswehr* administrative offices, which they managed to occupy, and then to two or three *Reichswehr* barracks, where they were told to go away or be machine-gunned. However, one stormtrooper unit succeeded in 'liberating' an arms cache of 3,000 old rifles, formerly used by the Munich home guard, in the cellar of a nunnery.

Otherwise Munich had a relatively peaceful night. The SA and *Kampfbund* men had been told that the next day, November 9, would be the great day of action; so they tried to snatch a few hours' rest at the Bürgerbräu and other meeting-places. Many probably dreamt of the 'march on Berlin' at which Hitler had hinted. The obvious geographical problems of the venture did not bother them.

But in Berlin the threat was not shrugged off as a silly idea. The Social-Democratic Prussian Minister of the Interior, Severing, and the creator and chief of the *Reichswehr,* General von Seeckt, had a row over it in the presence of Reichs President Ebert. They came to no decision what should be done to stop the rebels. As during the Kapp putsch, Seeckt warned again, '*Reichswehr* does not shoot at *Reichswehr,*' which now meant: if the Bavarian contingent of the German army sided with the rebels, marching with them on Berlin, then the Prussian contingent would not put up an armed resistance to defend the capital.

In fact, the Bavarian *Reichswehr* was already marching – or rather travelling – but in the opposite direction. Around midnight, telegrams from the Munich HQ had arrived in a number of Bavarian garrison towns, ordering a few thousand men by train to Munich to reinforce the garrison there. So while the rebels slept, the counter-revolution was rolling along at full speed.

After their release from the Bürgerbräu, Kahr, Lossow, and Seisser had first gone to their respective offices to find out whether the rebels had caused any mischief, and then they met again at the General State Commissariat in the town centre. Kahr, the aristocrat, and Lossow, the general, were still highly indignant at the arrogance with which they had been treated by that interloper of an Austrian corporal. They were determined to cut him down to size with all means at their disposal. Seisser needed a little more persuasion to agree that the 'word of honour' he had given to Hitler was null and void because it had been extorted.

At 1 am the three decided to play safe by moving their anti-putsch headquarters away from Kahr's office, where they might again be caught by the rebels, to the outlying barracks of the dependable Infantry Regiment 19 of the *Reichswehr*. From here, Lossow had this message transmitted at 3 am by the wireless-telegraph station:

> To all German wireless stations. General State Commissioner von Kahr, General von Lossow and Colonel von Seisser reject Hitler putsch. Agreement at Bürgerbräu meeting extorted by force of arms and therefore invalid. Beware of misuse of above names.

At 5.30 am the transmitter informed all Bavarian wireless stations:

> Situation in Munich: all barracks and important buildings firmly in hands of *Reichswehr* and Bavarian police. Reinforcements on the way.

An hour or so later, another message went out to the Bavarian authorities in the frontier regions:

> Strictest border checks to be enforced. Arrest all members of National-Socialist and allied organizations trying to escape. Signed: Kahr.

The putsch leaders suspected nothing. Some stormtrooper units rose early to start actions of their own such as arresting Social-Democratic town councillors as hostages, and wrecking the editorial offices of the Social-Democratic newspaper. The Munich telephone directory was scanned for Jewish-sounding names of businessmen; their bearers were dragged out of their beds, insulted, spat upon, knocked about, and threatened with shooting. Their homes were wrecked. It was an extemporized preview of what life in a Nazi state would be like.

At the Munich police headquarters, Dr Wilhelm Frick, a senior official and NSDAP member, had usurped the post of Chief of Police, declaring the old one deposed. Some career-conscious officials crowded around him and congratulated him. A few hours later, after a telephone order from Kahr, these same officials returned – to arrest him.

The way the rebel leaders spent the hours before their intended 'march on Berlin' shows the hopelessly amateurish nature of the whole enterprise. There was no information service which would have told Hitler during the night what he was up against so that he could have modified his plans accordingly. In fact, there were no plans at all, apart from a nebulous general idea of that march. So when they at last heard in the morning that a counter-offensive by the government forces was in full swing, they either did not believe it – how could the triumvirate break their word? – or they pooh-poohed it: Ludendorff, for one, was firmly convinced that no soldier or policeman would lift a finger against him, the great German war leader. The others, and most of all Hitler himself, put their trust in Hitler's ability to overcome any difficulty.

He, Goering, and Ludendorff wasted those hours discussing how to proceed. They had tried in vain to ring the triumvirate; they had sent messengers who were turned away or arrested. Ludendorff was now in favour of organizing a 'peaceful march' into town, only to the Marienplatz, in order to 'get the people on our side'. Goering prudently suggested 'withdrawing forces' to Rosenheim, his home town south-east of Munich, to await developments. But Hitler, in his Wagnerian mood, wanted his heroic climax, '*so oder so*', one way or the other, a favourite phrase of his. There must be an armed march, he insisted, and if necessary a battle. Eventually the others agreed, not without misgivings.

The sortie from the Bürgerbräu I had witnessed in the morning had been only a sideshow. Apart from the intimidating appearance of the SA in the town centre, the *Kampfbund* staged an attack on the police headquarters and failed – they probably did not know that Frick was no longer the new police chief but a prisoner. Now there were two thousand or so putschist 'troops' in town, armed with rifles, pistols, and machine-guns. Towards noon, they were formed into a marching column, with Hitler, Ludendorff, Röhm, Hess, and Goering at the head. Some SA units stayed behind at the Bürgerbräu because they were having an early lunch.

The road through the town centre seemed open to them; a poorly armed police unit was dispersed by the marchers. They reached the Marienplatz, still crowded with people who cheered them. A lorry with a machine-gun in position joined them on the way towards the former royal *Residenz*: a route which must have seemed logical to the leaders, for this was the road to the north, to the suburb of Schwabing and, five hundred miles further on, to Berlin. However, it turned out that the first quarter mile was the crucial stretch of the road.

A narrrow old street leads from the Marienplatz to the *Residenz,* which lies on the right. On the left is the *Feldherrnhalle,* the 'Hall of Generals', a replica of the *Loggia dei Lanzi* in Florence, put up by the Italophile King Ludwig I. Beyond the Hall and the *Residenz* lies a large square, the Odeonsplatz, leading into the very wide, northbound Ludwigstrasse. But the narrow passage between the *Residenz* and the *Feldherrnhalle* is a proper bottleneck, especially for a marching column.

Yet this was the road they had to take; the alternative route, through an equally narrow, parallel street to the Odeonsplatz, was already blocked by Seisser's Bavarian police. The column of the two thousand rebels was also squeezed by crowds of sympathizers marching on the footpaths of the narrow street, cheering and joining in their chauvinistic songs.

The marchers were just on the point of emerging into the Odeonsplatz when their first rows saw, right in front of them, a police unit, well armed with rifles, carbines, pistols, and rubber truncheons. Within seconds, there was a scrimmage: some of Hitler's men, brandishing pistols or rifles with bayonets, attacked the police, trying to push through. The policemen defended themselves with their rifle butts and truncheons.

No one could say for sure who fired the first shot, but it was most likely one of the marchers, for the first man who fell, killed by a bullet, was a policeman. More single shots followed, and then the police opened fire with a machine-gun they had quickly brought up from the rear.

Minutes later, the narrow street was empty except for the dead and wounded lying around. Rebels and sympathizers had fled in a panic: that was the end of the 'march on Berlin'. Only Ludendorff did not run away or seek cover; the old soldier, sure of the magic of his personality, marched on arrogantly, straight through the rows of shooting policemen – and into the arms of a lieutenant who took him into the *Residenz* as a prisoner.

Fourteen rebels, most of them young men, and four policemen including a captain lay dead. Hitler had thrown himself to the ground, hurting his shoulder, after the first exchange of shots; then he scrambled to his feet and tried to run behind the marchers, who were now in utter confusion. The chief doctor of the stormtroopers, who had parked his car in a side street, ran after him, put him in his car and drove him out of town, to the country villa of their friend 'Putzi' Hanfstaengl. Here, Hitler was arrested, on Kahr's orders, two days later. The putsch was over and Kahr the victor.

It was the first and last time Hitler was put behind bars, and there was some significance in the fact that this happened in Bavaria. In those days of inflation just before the putsch one could sense the growing trust in Hitler among the middle classes who were desperately looking for a saviour; but after the failed putsch it became clear that their attitude swung round: now he was to them a troublemaker who had caused unrest and casualties, to no purpose but the fulfilment of his own mad lust of power. Kahr, they felt, had been right to put an end to National Socialism in Bavaria; he was the proper guardian of bourgeois-conservative society, the kind of establishment our Bavarians liked best. National Socialism was practically dead in our neck of the German woods. Ten years later, when Hitler assumed power in Berlin, this antagonism explained why Bavaria was the *Land* that resisted the Nazi takeover the longest.

As to Ludendorff, Kahr put him firmly in his place. A day after the battle of the *Feldherrnhalle* I saw posters signed by him – politics by posters was still much in favour – which denounced the 'deceit and perjury of ambitious fellows', with whom 'the Prussian Ludendorff and his followers' had made common cause. So the mere adjective 'Prussian' was still a term of utter disapproval even in Bavaria's official idiom!

With the end of inflation a few days later, Kahr's own putsch plans fizzled out. His regime ended in the spring of 1924 as Germany was returning to a more or less normal life. Yet Hitler never forgot. On June 30, 1934, in the 'night of the long knives' which cost Röhm and a hundred other SA officers their lives, he also had old Kahr murdered, amongst many other victims of his hatred and revenge.

Goering had been wounded by a bullet in his hip at the *Feldherrnhalle* and stormtroopers carried him to the nearest doorway; it was a bank I knew well, and there they told me that a Jewish clerk had given Goering first aid. Then he, too, fled by car to friends in the country. After hiding for two days, he and his wife managed to cross the Austrian border; he remained in exile in Rome and Stockholm for nearly four years, returning to Germany only in 1927. Rudolf Hess, too, escaped to Austria but came back of his own free will and was arrested. Röhm had stayed on in Munich and surrendered to the *Reichswehr*.

Altogether, 216 putschists were caught, but only a handful were put in the dock at the trial which began on February 26, 1924.

Two months after the end of the inflation the Allies, led by the realistic Americans, gave us some solid hope that the question of reparations would now be solved once for all, making another blow-up of Germany's financial system unlikely. A commission headed by Charles Gates Dawes, President of a trust company in Chicago, with an American economist, Owen D. Young, and three British financial experts as its members, began the job of surveying Germany's situation and resources. The first result was a loan of hundreds of millions of gold mark to the German economy, which ushered in a period of optimism and prosperity. Under the Dawes Plan, as it was called, and later under the Young Plan, Germany was able to pay her debts to the Allies without too much hardship, thus removing from the Versailles Treaty its most dangerous sting.

At the same time when the Dawes-Young commission got down to work, the Hitler trial began before Munich's 'People's Court'. Everybody was wondering how the judges, traditionally a conservative or downright reactionary breed, would handle the tricky case in which the Austrian ex-corporal was to share the dock with the German war leader. Twice I succeeded in wangling my way into the public gallery; admission was severely restricted – the idea of justice having to be seen to be done had not yet taken root in Germany, and this awkward court case was certainly not meant to be a show trial.

It was obvious that the judges intended merely to go through the motions required by the letter of the law, and to let the accused off with the mildest possible sentences. Proceedings against some who ought to have been in the dock had already been dropped, not because of any sympathy with, or fear of Hitler, but out of regard for the top people who had backed him behind the scenes.

The accused were Hitler himself, Hess, Röhm, Frick, some minor Nazi functionaries, and Ludendorff. He had, after all, been caught red-handed, and it had been impossible not to charge him. I happened to be among the audience on the day he was allowed to make a long propaganda speech, spelling out his confused philosophy. He had been marching, he explained, against 'international Jewry' and the 'anti-German' Vatican – not a very effective argument in Bavaria with its three-quarters Roman-Catholic population. His political and general stupidity was palpable. I was amazed to hear the judges address this prisoner in the dock as 'Excellency'.

In striking contrast, Hitler displayed his instinctive political shrewdness. He never attempted to deny that he had committed high treason: 'I take the responsibility for all the consequences,' he said, 'but this does not mean that I'm a criminal. I don't feel like one – on the contrary!' He was well aware that this trial was his chance for a splendid propaganda exercise and he used it.

He, too, was allowed to speak for as long as he wanted throughout the 24 days of the trial, and his words were reported by the press all over Germany. He was, clearly, building up his image as the potential future saviour of the country.

'The army we have recruited,' he said in his final address to the court, 'is growing day by day and hour by hour with increasing speed. Especially now I have the proud hope that the moment will arrive when these wild swarms become battalions, the battalions regiments, the regiments divisions; when the old black, white, and red cockade will be retrieved from the mud, the old standards fly above the vanguard!'

This was no mere rhetoric; every newspaper reader knew what he meant: the war of revenge against the Allies, especially France, the arch enemy.

The verdicts and sentences (pronounced, appropriately enough, on April 1) were no surprise. Hitler and Hess got the minimum sentence for high treason, five years' detention in a fortress — the traditional place of confinement for 'honourable' offences (such as duels) in Germany — with the recommendation of release after less than a year. Röhm, Frick, and most of the other accused were given shorter prison sentences and released on probation.

Ludendorff was acquitted; pompous as he was, he protested vigorously: 'I regard this acquittal as a humiliation for the uniform and the decorations I am wearing!' he shouted. There were enthusiastic cries of *'Heil'* from the public gallery. 'I have to call Your Excellency to order,' said the presiding judge meekly. A posse of press photographers was waiting for him outside the court: he was still a more important man than Hitler.

The worst bit of arbitrariness which the court and the authorities committed was the complete neglect of the laws of the Weimar Republic, which required that a foreign national found guilty of high treason must be expelled. No one even suggested that this clause should be applied to Hitler.

Yet for the great majority of the people of Munich and Bavaria, his removal to the fortress of Landsberg was a good riddance. They were now more concerned with picking up the pieces of business after the enormous losses they had suffered in the inflation. The 'arch enemy' was coming to his senses: in the French elections, Poincaré suffered a crushing defeat, which meant the end of the Ruhr adventure and of all aspirations for the Rhineland. The Dawes Plan money which flowed into Germany also helped the recovery of the large industrial works in the Munich area. I think most of us thought it best to forget all that had happened in 1923.

We also forgot about Hitler. Only occasionally the papers told us that he was quite comfortably settled in his private

In his comfortable cell in the fortress of Landsberg, Hitler under a laurel wreath — a gift from sympathizers

room in the fortress, with pictures on the walls and flowers on the table, receiving visitors and talking to his fellow prisoner Rudolf Hess. He was also writing a book, it was said. In fact, it was Hess who advised him to use his time at Landsberg for that purpose, and start again working on a manuscript he had laid aside in 1922. Hitler dictated most of the book to Hess during the $8\frac{1}{2}$ months he spent in the fortress. It was to be called *Mein Kampf*.

He was released just in time to celebrate Christmas and toast the New Year, 1925, with his cronies. That year, however, started badly for him. First in Bavaria and then in Prussia and most of the rest of Germany he was banned from speaking in public. Then came a humiliating defeat for Ludendorff as the candidate of the NSDAP in the presidential elections.

In February, poor President Ebert had been dutifully attending to his work instead of having his appendicitis treated. The result was peritonitis and death. The Republic's first head of state, with his working-class background, had never presented the image of a statesman. Germany's right-wingers used every opportunity for turning him into a figure of fun, and even the Democratic *Berliner Illustrierte* did a ghastly thing to him. I remember our shocked amusement when that most popular of weeklies, in the summer before his death, spread an enlarged seaside snapshot of him in his funny old-fashioned bathing trunks all over its front page. That picture and that caption, *'Ebert in der Badehose',* made an honest but dull man the ridiculous symbol of our Republic.

Hitler would have liked to stand as a candidate for Ebert's succession, but he was still an Austrian citizen, widely barred from public speaking; so he put up Ludendorff — who got no more than one per cent of the votes against the candidate of the moderate nationalists, his former boss General Field Marshal Paul von Hindenburg. His election victory was indirectly a defeat of Hitler but, as it turned out nearly nine years later, a blessing in disguise for him. Hindenburg, 77, was the embodiment of middle and upper-class nostalgia for the good old days, though he was no more than a figure-head – 'A man in uniform with a lot of medals', as Stresemann called him. But now the *Reichswehr* had a supreme commander to whom it could look up in reverence, the provincial diehards had their father figure, and the caste of the *Junkers,* the big landowners, had one of their own breed at the head of the establishment. Hindenburg's election was a triumph of nationalism and militarism and a significant setback for the Republic and democracy.

I think it was in that year that Hitler also had a private mishap. I heard the story from a Jewish-orthodox friend. It must have been the first time that Hitler seriously contemplated marriage, and his bride-to-be was the sister of Ernst ('Putzi') Hanfstaengl, beautiful Erna, with whom he had begun a close relationship, no doubt also with an eye on the family's money. But inflation had left quite a cash problem for the art publishers, and they saw only one way of giving Erna a substantial dowry: selling a property they owned in Munich's Kanalstrasse. To his horror, Hitler learnt that on this site stood, of all things, the synagogue of the Jewish-orthodox congregation, who were prepared to buy it. What would Hitler's flock have said if it had transpired from what source he got his dowry? Anyway, the marriage project fell through.

5
THE WICKED AND WONDERFUL
METROPOLIS

The changing times put an end to our ancestral business. The site of the two-storey shacks right in the middle of Munich's commercial centre, which had housed the *Loden* coat manufacture for half a century, turned out to be a valuable property, worthy of something more modern and profitable than an old-fashioned factory. A slick, swarthy young man from Berlin came one day and offered a tidy sum for the site. He had been sent by one of the large film companies which were now flourishing in the capital and competing with each other in buying up existing cinemas or building new ones all over Germany as outlets for their own films. New cinemas were no longer built as fleapits but as show palaces, and now Munich, too, was to have one. There was already then, in 1926, a slight touch of megalomania in the German film industry — an infection which came, of course, from Hollywood.

My own film bug was still gnawing away, and after the swarthy young man had concluded the purchase of our factory site I asked him if he could get me a job, any job, in his Berlin company. To my surprise I got a letter inviting me to present myself to the chairman.

I went to Berlin like a shot, burning to start my career in the most fascinating industry on earth. I would, no doubt, get some job in a studio, learn the technical tricks of the trade, and end up as a famous film director. What I got, however, was the grossly underpaid position of an assistant receptionist at an old but luxurious cinema on the Kurfürstendamm, recently acquired by the company. That was my evening job; during the day, I had to help writing the story-sheets which the distribution department supplied to provincial cinemas.

It was all rather disappointing, but at least I had the chance of rubbing shoulders with famous film people. Alas, my attempt at establishing contact with a director failed because the girl I used as a go-between turned out to be not a hopeful starlet but a hopeless con-woman who got an expensive outfit of clothes from a top fashion house and had the bill sent to the director. The police were called. I was traced back as the fellow who had been gullible enough to bring director and swindler together. I found myself out on my ears, one of the growing mass of Berlin's unemployed. But I was also one of the many 'new' Berliners who, once they had tasted the exhilarating flavour of Germany's capital in the mid-1920s, were determined to stay on, despite the difficulty of finding jobs.

A latecomer among the world's capitals, Berlin had begun its vigorous growth in the 1870s, founders' years, when all Central Europe sent its most enterprising sons to the new imperial metropolis with its great business opportunities. Now, as Germany was recovering from war and inflation, Berlin attracted, most of all, the artists and intellectuals from the provinces with their limited chances for such people. Many also came from the east and south-east: some were simply seeking freedom, others were fed up with the stagnating atmosphere of their home towns which, such as Vienna or Budapest, had come down in the cultural world. One might say that the capital of the Weimar Republic was a kind of Central European New York.

Berlin had about four million inhabitants, and almost 150,000 of them were foreigners. The very attraction of the town added to its main disadvantage, high unemployment. Yet, strangely enough, this did not seem to impede its phenomenal rise to Europe's and perhaps the world's capital of art and culture, which was just about to begin when I settled there.

The first two years of my life as a Berliner, after my short spell in the film world, were typical of thousands of other jobless middle-class youngsters — drifting from one attempt at making ends meet to another, helping out in an uncle's office, trying to sell shopkeepers goods they did not want; playing the piano as background music to silent films for a sandwich and three marks per evening. In the end, however, I was luckier than most: I became the Berlin correspondent of a Munich newspaper-publishing group. I learnt the trade of a journalist as I went along, and my relationship to Berlin changed completely. I was no longer an outsider desperately trying to merge into its life – I was an independent observer watching people and events, equipped with a press card, the magic wand that opened every 'No Admission' door to me; I could meet anybody I wanted to interview, from film star to cabinet minister. I had a vantage point from which I could witness what was going on.

And there was an immense range of things going on, though we Berliners had little idea, at the time, how far-reaching, how long-lasting these trends and developments were to be.

The first thing I learnt was the curious social geography of the town, the result of the combined or conflicting forces of ancient royal planning and latter-day industrial growth, class segregation and commercialization, the tendency towards exclusivity among the old upper crust and towards gregarious jollity among the *nouveaux riches*. Berlin's working classes preferred to stay in their strictly defined areas, such as the 'Wedding': rows and rows of enormous tenement houses, each with a sunless yard at the back leading to another or several more tenement blocks. It was a dirty, neglected, noisy, grey, and poor habitat for what were then the underdogs of society. We, the bourgeoisie, had practically no contact with them.

Our world was the Westend, with the wide, busy Kurfürstendamm as its axis. Here were the most attractive shops, some of the town's best theatres, the largest cinemas, the most famous cafés and restaurants, and many (for us young men very convenient) small hotels for spending an hour or a night with one's girl, and no questions asked.

It was, in fact, Berlin's Westend which quickly became, in the minds of those who appreciated or hated everything it stood for, synonymous with 'Weimar'. The idyllic little town of that name in Thuringia contributed nothing but its accidental role as the birthplace of Germany's republican constitution to all the affection, contempt, and later nostalgia the name of Weimar evoked.

In the German provinces, however, 'Berlin' was a most hateful term. Their almost neurotic antagonism against the wicked metropolis was also a geographical misunderstanding. They did not mean the City with its businesses and offices, not the Wilhelmstrasse with its ministerial mansions, not the Wedding with its proletarian life. They meant the Westend when they called Berlin a foreign capital, a sinful, un-German town. It

The gigolo, hired by lonely ladies as a dancing partner: a typical character of the 1920s

was the excesses and dissipations of Berlin in the inflation which had got stuck in the provincial minds; the image remained, and they still saw the town as a centre of libertinism, vice, and ostentatious frivolity. A new term was all that had to be added in the late 1920s to the glossary of abuse for Berlin's cultural achievements — *Kulturbolschewismus*. Grudgingly and enviously, they watched the town's growing appreciation abroad.

Significantly, all the Nazi leaders who were to occupy the Wilhelmstrasse in 1933 came from the provinces.

For most young people who had settled in Berlin its image was rather different. The very air of the town was exciting, there was something new every day; the encouraging fresh trends of post-war Germany which I had experienced in Munich seemed to be coming to fruition now in Berlin. Perhaps the whole country's regeneration would spread from here?

But we who lived in the Westend deluded ourselves, perhaps deliberately. In our enthusiasm and optimism we ignored the nasty features of the town, obvious and obtrusive though they were. We did not take in the contrast between the glitter of the Kurfürstendamm and the grinding poverty of the jobless in the working-class districts because we never looked beyond the Westend. We saw, and did not want to see, the many prostitutes sharing the sidewalks with the blind and limbless war veterans who sat, begging, propped up against the walls. We laughed about the obese profiteers and their overdressed ladies gorging enormous, cream-topped *gâteaux* at the pavement tables of the cafés, and looked away from the hungry faces of kids in rags who were trotting by, sometimes rummaging in the litter bins for food thrown away. We met them all again in the caustic cartoons of George Grosz and the haunting drawings of Käthe Kollwitz, which we appreciated without true compassion.

An evil that was spreading fast in Berlin was drug-taking. It was mostly cocaine, called *Koks* in the vernacular, which was used as a stimulant, usually being snuffed. The next step would be morphine jabs. My first experience with cocaine had been in Munich; a young homosexual, the brother of a popular film actor, took me and a couple of friends of mine, all aged about fifteen, to his flat and let us snuff the white powder in the hope of making us addicts and dependent on him. Fortunately, the stuff did nothing whatsoever to us. Later, in Berlin, I saw it being sold and snuffed in the shadier night clubs, despite severe penalties for the dealers and users if they were caught. The police had special drug squads with detectives touring the Westend.

So there was something in that provincial image of a sick and sordid metropolis after all. There was even more in the charge that it was a den of unabashed perversity. Certainly a large sector of the entertainment business came within that category. One went, for instance, to night spots like the *Eldorado* to watch men in drag dancing together, or to the *Mali und Igel* for a glimpse of lesbian sex *chez soi*. Straightforward homosexual bars and cafés abounded; the classiest was the *Wunderbar*, where prominent actors met in tastefully decorated surroundings, not in the least worried about giving themselves away as homosexuals by their mere presence. It fulfilled, like most others of its kind, a definite social function as a meeting-place, as well as being part of Berlin's show business.

The police rarely interfered, although the penal code of the Republic still had its notorious clause 175 prohibiting intercourse between males (lesbians were, as in other western countries, not mentioned by the law). But there were places, especially around the Alexanderplatz in the east, where homosexuality and real crime went, so to speak, hand in hand: low-grade bars in which the visitor, more often than not a provincial tourist, was likely to be relieved of his wallet or blackmailed.

If it was a bout of whipping you wanted, the whores parading around the largest Westend department store would gratify your desire. They wore high, bright-red riding-boots as an advertisement for their speciality, and some used to carry short whips in order to narrow any margin of doubt to a minimum. I also heard of private circles indulging in other kinds of perversion; one, whose members were mainly officers and aristocrats, was said to be devoted to coprophagia: a prostitute was hired and paid for eating only chocolate for three days, then given a laxative; the gentlemen would gather around and feast on her excreta, with her belly as their dinner table.

All this was part of a distasteful world with which we, the bourgeois youth, had nothing to do. Our idea of sex was very different; in fact, I think that sex was discovered not in England and America by the young people of the 1960s but by us in Berlin in the 1920s.

The claim may sound eccentric; there are, however, some good reasons for it. For Germany, the First World War was a more radical break between two eras than for any other country except Russia, particularly for the middle classes who had been the backbone of German society. They had developed a social, ecomomic and moral tradition which was not much older than the Hohenzollern empire and therefore not rooted as deeply and firmly as in the older European nations. The lost war and the disaster of inflation confused and disrupted the middle-class way of life – its *Weltanschauung,* its basic concepts and its rules of behaviour.

Our generation welcomed the upheaval, for we had witnessed and to some extent suffered from the inherent hypocrisy of our parents' way of life. The 'generation gap' was to us then not what it is today – a sociological term for lack of mutual understanding – but a tangible reality. Out of our contempt for that hypocrisy, in our refusal to accept the shambles of a bankrupt morality, we tried to develop some sort of a new

Weltanschauung, shaky and vague, as we passed through puberty into early adulthood. In that phase, when sex is the most powerful emotional and intellectual impulse, we enjoyed it wholeheartedly, just because it had been a matter the previous generation used to sweep under the carpet, secretly practising something very different from what they were sanctimoniously preaching.

(right) Frank Wedekind, the author of *Spring's Awakening* and *Lulu* (drawing by Th.Th. Heine). He also wrote many songs which he sang in the cabarets, accompanying himself on the lute

(left) An early title page of the satirical journal, *Simplicissimus,* designed by Th.Th. Heine

There were outward phenomena which seemed to us characteristic of that break. For instance, girls acquired legs. It must have been the war work in which women had taken part in Germany as well as in England, and which made the pre-war ankle-length skirts a major hindrance. Hemlines began to move up first in 1915, and by the end of the war the short skirt was well established. It had also come to stay because women needed it for various kinds of sport they were now taking up and, last but not least, for dancing the new way, the jazz way. Dancing grew into almost a mania, culminating in the Charleston which certainly demanded short skirts: by 1926, the girls' knees became visible, at least for a year or so.

This may have influenced the change of men's favourite type of girls. It was no longer the child-like, well-behaved virgin; nor was it in Germany the 'bright young thing' of English post-war society. Our favourite was the *garçonne,* the independent, knowing, self-reliant woman who, as a rule, had her own career (and income): an equal partner in love as well as in mind. Age was acquiring a new kind of importance; youth was the age for trying out relationships and acquiring experience, early marriages were somewhat out of favour. The ideal couple was the mature man of, say, forty and the sensitive and sensible woman in her early thirties.

We sang and danced to a very popular 'hit' by the young song-writer Friedrich Hollaender, which chimed to perfection with our romantic-realistic idea of sex: 'Johnny, I like your birthday best, then I will be your guest for all the night . . .'

Still, we might have been fighting a losing battle against the old moralists who kept calling us to order – parents, teachers, publicists – had we not found eminent guidance from men with a philosophy impossible to disregard because it was based on scientific perceptions.

I had never heard the name of Sigmund Freud in Munich. When I came to Berlin, however, the teachings of the bearded Viennese sage were all the rage there. Everybody was talking about the subconscious, about infantile sexuality, about libido, repression, superego, Freudian slips; many discovered in themselves some complex or neurosis, went to psychoanalysts and indulged in telling dreams and revealing mental associations. The number of practising analysts increased

97

almost daily; their main training centre was the Freudian Psychoanalytical Institute in Berlin, I think the first such establishment founded outside Vienna. Berlin was, no doubt, the most fertile soil for the new science, not because life in that town produced more neurotics than anywhere else, but because this was a completely fresh departure from the conventional concepts of what interested our post-war generation intensely: our own minds, our desires, our sex life.

Now we knew that the forbidden land of previous generations was nothing to be afraid of, that it was unhealthy to repress one's impulses, absurd to feel guilty about them. Our girls began to understand that the traditional hard-to-get attitude of the female was no longer *de rigueur*; modern science allowed her to enjoy love-making, and even expected her to have orgasms. Thus it was with the help of Freud that we discovered sex.

Of course, much of the Freudian craze was quite a ridiculous, ephemeral fashion. Yet a solid sediment remained: we were no longer floundering among the wreckage of yesterday's morality, we had found terra firma on which to build a new system of values — at least in one important sector of human activities.

Our literary idols nodded assent. Thomas Mann even apologized for having written something 'strongly anti-analytical' in his *Death in Venice,* explaining his *faux pas* as a 'characteristic example of repression'; but he had made up for it by creating a psychoanalyst as a character in his latest novel, *The Magic Mountain.* 'He may be slightly comic,' admitted Thomas Mann, 'but his comic touch is perhaps merely the author's indemnification for the deeper concessions to psychoanalysis which he makes within his works.' And Hermann Hesse wrote from his Swiss hideout about the 'fruitfulness' of Freud's teachings for the writer: 'We have here one more key — not a magic one, but a valuable new attitude, an excellent new tool whose usefulness and reliability have stood the test.'

Our enormous interest in the new psychology extended to Freud's pupils, rivals and opponents. Adler with his 'individual psychology', Jung with his 'collective unconscious', Wilhelm Reich with his over-riding emphasis on orgasm (he even invented an elementary particle involved in it, the 'orgon'): like the leaders of sects, they all found their circles of followers and believers.

Then there was Dr Magnus Hirschfeld with his first 'Institute of Sexual Science'; Berliners called him 'Auntie Magnesia' because he lectured about homosexuality with grave scientific seriousness. His aim was to enlighten the general public by means of books, journals, films, and open days at the Institute. I went along to one of these evenings. The large hall was crowded although the subject to be dealt with was never announced beforehand. Dr Karl Abraham, Hirschfeld's chief assistant, announced the subject from the rostrum: it was to be transvestism. He did not just lecture on it, he had brought a live specimen – a simple Berlin worker who had become a patient at the Institute. The poor man did not know what had hit him, what forced him to put on a woman's blouse under his overall and a bra under his vest. Obligingly, he undressed on the platform and showed us his surfeit of garments. Abraham discussed the problem with him; the audience listened in complete silence, fascinated. My editor, in Catholic Munich, refused to print my story about that evening.

Almost as famous as Freud's name was that of a Dutch doctor, Van de Velde, author of the most overt book about sex ever published until that time: *The Perfect Marriage*. Its main attraction was a detailed list of all imaginable copulative positions. Jokes about Van de Velde abounded among the Berliners, but I know definitely that the good doctor did save one or two tottering marriages among my friends. Jokes were also made about the equally frank book written – of all people – by a senior Medical Officer of the town. It had the title, *Masturbation: Neither Ailment nor Vice,* to which the Berliners added, '. . . but fun'.

Our attitude to sex was, I think, a well-balanced mixture of that 'new realism', the everyday philosophy which reflected our break with the past, and simple, old-fashioned romanticism – kisses at street corners, holding hands in the underground train, evenings in the woods around Berlin, nights in a small hotel or a bedsitter with subdued lights. In fact, we hardly ever used the word sex; we called it *Erotik,* a term with a slightly different flavour than its English equivalent. It meant to us the sublimation of the sex drive into a romantic state of mind, its elevation

Erich Kästner

Kästner at work in the café.
Cartoon by H. M. Brockmann

to a power from which true love might stem as well as artistic sensitivity and creativity. In a way it was a return to the romantic period of the early nineteenth century with its emotional intensity in art, music, and literature, especially poetry. But where was the poet of our own era?

He came in the late twenties. He was Erich Kästner, the son of a saddler from Dresden; he had studied to become a teacher but was disgusted by the excess of discipline and lack of imagination which were characteristic of Wilhelminian education. So after serving in the war he moved to Berlin as a freelance writer.

Kästner virtually bowled us over with his first verse volumes (which appeared in 1928/29, almost simultaneously with his brilliant thriller for children, *Emil and the Detectives*). There we had our young poet who felt and thought exactly as we did, and lent expression to his contemporaries' emotions and joys, concerns and fears with the same precision and wit as only Heine had done in German literature a century earlier. His realism and romanticism were our very own mixture. 'Since Kästner,' wrote a leading literary critic, 'people are reading poetry again.'

Kästner took a new look at our world and us in it. Poets, for instance, had always eulogized the spring; his viewpoint of the annual event was somewhat different:

> Most of the girls have started feeling shy.
> Like sweetened cream the blood runs in their veins.
> The sky is filled with shining aeroplanes.
> And you are happy. And you don't know why. . .
> . . . The same thing happens every single year.
> Yet every time it seems quite fundamental.
>
> (Translated by Eva Geisel)

But there was another important side to Kästner's *Gebrauchslyrik,* his 'poetry for everyday usage', as it was called. Like Heine before him, he was deeply worried about Germany, about certain features of her national character. In his poem *The Alternative* he said bluntly:

> If we had won the war – good heavens! –
> with iron fists and flags unfurled,

101

all Germany'd be at sixes and sevens
and look like a madhouse to the world. . .
. . . Then Reason would be kept in fetters,
and forced, at court, to kiss the rod.
New fights would be run like operettas
if we had won the war — thank God,
we didn't win it after all.

One of Kästner's most famous poems warned us, with almost
uncanny foresight, of the shape of things to come. Here are a
few lines (in John Lehmann's translation):

Knowst thou the land where only cannons grow?
Not heard of it? You'll know it soon, prepare!
There Jacks in office, keen as mustard, go
smartly to work as on a barrack square.

A corporal's collar under each cravat.
Faces galore but not a single head.
They dream of helmets when they sport a hat,
and make more soldiers when they go to bed . . .

. . . Knowst thou the land? All sorrows it could heal,
it could be happy and bring happiness.
A land of rolling cornfields, coal and steel,
and skilled and willing hands, all things that bless . . .

. . . There freedom withers, with no sun to nourish,
and when they build — it's one more barrack square.
Knowst thou the land where only cannons flourish?
Not heard of it? You'll know it soon, prepare!

Kästner was no ivory-tower poet. He was part of, and took
part in Berlin's life. He did not write in the traditional poet's attic
but in his local café, where we could watch him working and
sipping black coffee and staring out of the window in search of
a rhyme. The waiter carried his trays almost on tiptoe past Herr
Dr Kästner's table.

Every intellectual, artist, or run-of-the-mill bohemian had his

'Shut up and keep serving' was George Grosz' caption for his controversial pacifist drawing of Christ with gas mask and army boots

Stammcafé. The largest and most famous of these haunts was the 'Romanische' (so called because of its fake-Romanesque architecture) at the atrociously pretentious Kaiser-Wilhelm memorial church which marked the eastern end of the Kurfürstendamm. The Romanische was the Berlin equivalent of those other Continental cafés like the Central in Vienna or the Dôme in Paris where groups of political emigrants used to meet before the First World War. Once the Tsarist Foreign Minister in St Petersburg sent an angry note to his opposite number in Imperial Vienna, protesting about the machinations of the Russian emigrants in the Austro-Hungarian capital. The Minister read the note, shook his head and said sarcastically to his secretary, 'Who do they think will start a revolution in Russia – perhaps that Herr Trotsky from the Café Central?'

The Romanische, however, did not have such a marked political atmosphere, though most of the regulars tended, by nature of their professions, to the left. They enjoyed the intellectual freedom of the Republic, including the freedom to criticize its shortcomings, its social injustices, its lame stand against reaction. George Grosz, the era's best-known cartoonist who attacked militarism and capitalism with acid ruthlessness, had his circle at the café, which included Max Slevogt and Emil Orlik; here, Grosz' 'Christ on the Cross' – with gas mask and army boots — passed from hand to hand while he was defending himself in court against a charge of blasphemy.

Among the writers at the Romanische were, on and off, Heinrich Mann, Thomas's brother, Bert Brecht, Carl Zuckmayer, Joseph Roth, and occasionally foreign visitors such as Dorothy Thompson, Sinclair Lewis, Thomas Wolfe. The younger generation of film-makers at the café included Billy Wilder and Robert Siodmak; Anita Berber, the dancer, and her admirers had a separate table. There were art dealers and editors, radio personalities and publishers, musicians and conductors, actors and producers, lawyers and architects, and of course bohemian hangers-on who went from table to table scrounging cups of coffee and frankfurters with potato salad. The hardiest of them all, a failed poet and drug addict, was once asked what he thought would happen to him if the Nazis came to power. He shrugged and grinned: 'Scroungers will always be needed.'

When the Nazis did come to power the Romanische faded out quickly as a meeting place of Berlin's intellectuals and artists. My last visit was when I had an appointment with a Russian friend, a chemist who had developed a new process for copying leaflets. He brought his bulging attaché case along, full of anti-Nazi leaflets, which I took over for clandestine distribution. Outside, the stormtroopers marched across the square, and I didn't feel very heroic carrying something that would have landed me straight away in the Oranienburg concentration camp or the interrogation basement at the SS headquarters. Fortunately, no one paid much attention to just another oddball leaving the Romanische, and I got safely home.

The array of Germany's cultural workers — including, of course, those who were too esoteric to mix with their colleagues in cafés — was very large and diversified, and it was most enjoyable to live amongst them. At the time, however, we never guessed how powerful and long-lasting the impact of their achievements and ideas would be, nor that it would, strangely enough, affect the outside world most strongly when Weimar culture was given the death blow in Germany itself.

The first and perhaps the most influential movement of the

period did not start in Berlin but actually in the town of Weimar. There, the Berlin-born son of an architect, thirty-four year-old Walter Gropius, founded a school of applied art and architecture in 1918. He called it the *Bauhaus,* the House of Building. But it was very much more, covering every branch of designing and applied-art training. Within a few years, his ideas and principles turned out to be so radical and revolutionary that the good people of the town were scandalized and suggested to Gropius and his crowd that they move somewhere else. Another medium-sized community, Dessau in Saxony, offered them a roof over their heads; the place was already highly industrialized, in contrast to countryfied, old-world Weimar, and this suited the *Bauhaus* people quite well. They settled there in 1926, and from then on the term *Bauhaus Dessau* grew into a household word all over Germany, and eventually all over the world.

The very building they erected for their studios and workshops, designed in the new style, created a minor sensation: a simple, square, perfectly proportioned block of concrete, steel and glass, a functional house without any superfluous frills – the kind of building which has ever since been and still is being put up in all countries, a thoroughly familiar and therefore unexciting sight today. But the mere fact that, although this style was created over half a century ago, it keeps looking 'modern' to us speaks for itself.

The Berliners were a little jealous that such a unique new movement was centred on a provincial town, but its ideas were eagerly accepted in the capital. Gropius was now heading a whole group of devoted architects, designers, painters, sculptors, craftsmen, art teachers, and students, who all believed in the necessity of a new start in man's surroundings. Here was the visual 'new realism' to which our generation was already emotionally attuned.

'Modern man who wears modern clothes, not period costumes,' wrote Gropius, 'also needs a modern habitat with everyday utensils compatible with our time. Objects are determined by their functional nature; in order to make them serve us properly – a chair, a container, a house – that nature must first be studied. They must suit their purposes perfectly; they must be durable, inexpensive, and good-looking. . . . Whether we are architects, artists, or sculptors, we must all return to the crafts. There is no essential difference between the artist and the craftsman. Let us all forget snobbish distinctions!'

A typical example of a *Bauhaus* innovation was the first tubular chair, designed by Marcel Breuer. Ludwig Mies van der Rohe, a master-mason's son from Aachen near the Belgian border, who had studied with Gropius and Le Corbusier in Berlin, designed the first glass skyscraper at the *Bauhaus* as early as 1920, starting a new trend which is still alive in our time. 'We reject all aesthetic speculation, all doctrine, all formalism,' he said in a manifesto. 'Architecture is the will of the epoch translated into space. Living. Changing. New. Not the yesterday, only the today can be given form.'

Among the famous artists who worked at the *Bauhaus* as teachers were Paul Klee, Oskar Schlemmer, the New Yorker Lyonel Feininger, the Russian Vassily Kandinsky, the Hungarian Laszlo Moholy-Nagy (stage and metal designing, photography and typography). They came from many countries and they emigrated to many countries when the Hitler regime closed down the *Bauhaus* (in Berlin, where the group had moved in the last year of the Republic). They took its ideas and ideals with them; thus their reputation, and that of the whole movement, became even greater in the world when the *Bauhaus* itself had ceased to exist.

The East Prussian Erich Mendelsohn was probably the most prolific *Bauhaus* architect. During the war, in the trenches, he had filled his notebooks with sketches of what and how he would like to build. A decade later, we began to see his creations rise all over Berlin – in the newspaper district he designed one of the largest publishing houses, in East Berlin the headquarters of the Metal Workers' Union, opposite the Romanische Café the town's biggest and most impressive cinema, in the western residential suburbs vast modern blocks of flats. Mendelsohn was *the* architect of the new Berlin.

In 1919, still unknown, he had been entrusted with a formidable task which demanded architectural vision, scientific understanding, and technical knowledge: the building of the Einstein Institute in Potsdam, well outside the industrial belt of

Berlin because it was to be used, among other research work, for astronomical observations and needed clean air. The Einstein Tower, as it became to be known, looked like an oversize fairground slide topped by a giant Roman legionary's helmet – the movable dome of the observatory. One newspaper called the whole structure 'a cross between a New York skyscraper and a pyramid'. Nothing like it had ever been built, and its flowing lines of concrete seemed to epitomize the new age of astrophysics in contrast to the nearby redbrick building of the old observatory, Prussian style.

Certainly Einstein himself was a most unusual character among the traditional cast of German scientists. No one outside the physicists' circles had heard anything about him until he got the Nobel Prize in 1921, but then everybody was talking about that strange Theory of Relativity of his, formulated in his papers of 1905 and 1916, and largely confirmed by observations during the total eclipse of the sun in 1919.

One should have thought that after the Nobel award all Germany would hail Einstein as one of her most brilliant sons: the country had just lost a world war, but he had won for it the greatest scientific honour. Instead of gratitude and recognition he got defamation – from his own fellow scientists, and for no other reason than that of being a Jew. An organization of German Natural Scientists was set up, backed by the same people that had been behind the Kapp putsch, offering money to anyone who would write or speak against Einstein and his theory. Mass meetings were held for that purpose in the larger German towns; in Berlin the anti-Einstein clique hired the biggest concert hall. Einstein himself went along, unannounced, to listen to their tirades against him. He burst into laughter at the more absurd statements, and clapped his hands in mock applause, thus lashing his enemies to even greater fury. 'That was most amusing,' he said at the end. Years later, a hundred Nazi professors ganged up against him and published a book condemning his Theory of Relativity. 'Were I wrong,' quipped Einstein, '*one* professor would have been quite enough.'

Political interference with German science bordered on the ridiculous during the Weimar era. Max Planck, too, had published his Quantum Theory – the other pillar of our modern concept of the physical world – in the early years of the century, and got the Nobel Prize before Einstein; but being an 'Aryan' German he was spared the enmity of those of his fellow scientists whose envy took, wherever applicable, the form of anti-semitism. I interviewed Planck for my paper and found him a quiet, somewhat stiff old gentleman whom I could not persuade to talk much about his work. He told me, however, that he was on very friendly terms with Einstein, twenty years his junior, who would sometimes come to dinner carrying his violin, and after dinner the two would play sonatas, with Planck at the piano.

Soon after my visit to Planck at his large, old-fashioned house in a Berlin suburb I saw Einstein, and his Tower, for the first time. True to his informal, unsnobbish temperament he had invited the public to a popular lecture at the Potsdam institute. We enjoyed it no end. Einstein was a smiling, jolly man in his fifties, with a greying, unkempt mane and a dark, bushy moustache. He had not manuscript of his lecture, but spoke freely and in everyday language about some everyday phenomena to which we had never given much thought. Why, he asked, do the tea leaves in a cup, after stirring, gather in a tiny whirlpool in the centre of the surface? Why, when we go sailing on a mountain lake, does the wind suddenly drop around five pm? He told us. I forget his explanations, but the great thing was that this world-famous scientist bothered to enlighten us, and obviously enjoyed doing it. There was no word about astrophysics or relativity.

I paid a visit to his home after making sure that he was out at the time; it was to be an interview with his wife Elsa about the great man *en pantoufles,* a journalistic fashion at the time. Elsa received me at their top-floor flat in the Haberlandstrasse, a quiet little street in south-west Berlin. For Einstein as well as for Elsa this was their second marriage. Oddly enough, he had first married the daughter of a Serb peasant in 1903; he had met Mileva as a fellow student in Switzerland, and they had two sons. But they were too dissimilar to stay together, and after several years the marriage ended in divorce. In 1919, he married Elsa, a distant cousin and a widow with two daughters; like him, she came from a provincial Jewish community in southern Germany. It was a happy, comfortable marriage. 'I'm glad my wife doesn't know anything about science,' he used to say. 'My first wife did.'

Frau Elsa showed me around. The professor's study, she said, was out of bounds to her, even for dusting. She seemed quite unimpressed by his fame and all the honours bestowed on him; she was at least as proud of the little clay figures, mostly of animals, made by her daughter Margot – the flat was full of them.

Then she took me up to the attic, which was mainly used as a store room; but there was a nice old telescope at the window. 'So this is where the professor observes the stars,' I said. 'Oh no,' she said. 'That telescope belonged to my first husband. He was a grain dealer, but astronomy was his hobby.'

There was no shortage of great men in Berlin in the 1920s; the town was a journalist's paradise. Everything new, important, remarkable seemed to be happening in the German capital – the envy of the provinces was understandable. But we also had our fair share of scandals, of humbug and charlatanism, typical of the time, and splendid fodder for the printing presses.

Superstition, pseudo-religion, sects had their heyday in Berlin's hectic atmosphere. Here, Buddhism got its first foothold in the western world, with a temple and a suburban community settlement. The more exotic and eccentric a sect was, the greater was its snob value. Reluctantly, I had to part with a girl friend of mine when she became a follower of Mazdaism, an offspring of the Zoroaster cult, which entailed a lavish consumption of garlic. Young husbands and wives embraced a new Italian creed called Carezza; it required *coitus sublimatus* as the basis of married life (with an erroneous reference to Dr Marie Stopes): the sex act begins as usual, but then 'freezes' – there must be no movement and no orgasm, but 'sublime, pure, poetical, divine happiness' instead.

Astrologers and clairvoyants had a great time. Hitler had his own astrologer called Elsbeth Ebertin. Berlin's most famous clairvoyant, a Czechoslovak Jew who called himself Hanussen, succeeded in getting the rich and influential as his clientele, and even some Nazi leaders consulted him. However, his renowned powers of foretelling the future failed in his own case, or he would not have ventured alone into the Grunewald forest the day the SS were waiting there to murder him.

Con-men abounded. Once I followed up the report that

German industry was pouring large sums into the 'secret' project of an analytical chemist who had discovered a way of running internal-combustion engines on water instead of petrol. The story sounded fishy, to say the least. I got the man to receive me at his laboratory near Berlin. How he made his 'discovery' work was, of course, a precious secret – he was just about to get his patent, he said – but he demonstrated to me a car which was 'running on water'. Even to a layman like myself the whole thing was obviously a swindle. I just reported what I saw. Four weeks later the man was arrested. The most incredible feature about the scheme was, as the trial revealed, that the biggest industrial companies had been conned by the simple device of bribing their experts sent to evaluate the discovery – they got half of what their firms invested in it. Only one of them had been honest and informed the police.

Another famous case, which left a good many Berliners with rather red faces, was that of a mineral water tapped, bottled, and sold with enormous publicity. It was supposed to cure practically every ailment from gout and gallstones to heart trouble and hayfever. The advertisements included a chemical analysis of the water as well as unsolicited testimonials by users who swore to its great healing powers. Countless millions of bottles were sold until an independent chemist took the trouble of analysing Berlin's ordinary tap water to see what the difference was. There was none. It turned out that the makers got their 'mineral' water from wells very near those feeding the Berlin water system, and just added a modicum of carbon dioxide to make it fizzy.

In fact, the 1920s were a golden age of gullibility. Miracle healers gathered flocks of paying believers round them with the greatest of ease; the most spectacular character among them was a 70-year-old former sergeant-major in the Kaiser's army, Josef Weissenberg. He called himself, somewhat modestly, a 'mesmerizer', but to his thousands of followers he was the 'Divine Master' and his sect the 'New Jerusalem'. For many years, Weissenberg never failed to provide the newspapers with sensational stories – and the authorities with unusual problems.

Families refused to have their dead buried but knelt around them, fervently praying for their resurrection under the guidance of the Divine Master. Housewives had to be carted off to lunatic asylums after spells under Weissenberg's influence; one of them tried to saw off her own arm. There were hysterical scenes at the Criminal Court whenever he appeared as a defendant, which happened several times; he always got off scot-free, escorted in triumph from the court by crowds of female believers. His healing panacea was cream cheese, slightly salted. A man suffering from a carbuncle died after treatment with cheese – daubed on the sore spot, not eaten; a baby with an eye infection went totally blind. Yet there was not enough evidence for convicting the Divine Master. It was said that the number of his followers was 100,000.

I visited the 'Peace Town New Jerusalem' he had established in the sandy hills south of Berlin, a village with rows of bungalows, an old people's home, an assembly hall, workshops, a coffee-house and a beer-garden, plus a dairy farm for the supply of cream cheese. He treated us press men to a roll-call of the residents, at which he appeared in his old uniform with decorations under the former imperial flag. There was a museum with paintings of a 'trance artist', a room furnished entirely with pieces made from antlers, life-size coloured photographs of the Divine Master as a grenadier, and a stuffed pug. The 'church' had a wrought-iron altar and larger-than-life wooden models of Weissenberg, Jesus Christ, and a couple of angels, all in white garments. Here, the 'sisters', or female members of the community, went into trances with screaming, eye-rolling, and convulsions; some were writhing in obscene movements and shouting 'in tongues'. It seemed to me like a Breughel picture brought to ghastly life.

In the end the law got Weissenberg for yet another fatal cream-cheese treatment, but he died before starting his prison term. New Jerusalem disintegrated: and those who needed that king of emotional outlet found it in the rallies of another political 'sect' headed by an ex-NCO – National Socialism.

Strange things, which should have been understood as warning signals, were going on in the provinces. But we ignored them; seen from Berlin, they merely confirmed to us what we already knew: that the greater part of Germany, and in particular of its middle and upper classes, had no taste for concepts and ideals like democracy, parliamentarism, civil liberties. To them, the Republic was a superfluous experiment that had, predictably, failed. On our island Berlin we still hoped that our *Weltanschauung,* our forward-looking, internationally orientated way of life might win over those narrow-minded, chauvinistic provincials, yesterday's men, in the end; that time was on our side. It wasn't.

Some affairs, ominous as they were, looked to us just ridiculous, such as that of the fake Hohenzollern Prince, Harry Domela. He was a lad from the Baltic provinces whose family had vanished during the war and its aftermath. He enlisted with the 'Baltic Volunteer Corps', that notorious band of raffish mercenaries, organised in 1919 by the Baltic *Junkers* to fight the Bolsheviks. For a time it was a grand life for young Domela – drinking, whoring, marching, shooting. When the *Junkers'* dream of reconquering their lands ended, the mercenaries were transferred to the west to help suppress the workers' revolts that were flaring up in various parts of Germany in the first years of the Republic; inevitably, the Corps was drawn into the Kapp putsch. When it failed, the Corps was disbanded, and Domela was left to walk the streets of Berlin, a 16-year-old boy without a home, a family, a job, or an aim in life. He tried his luck in all kinds of work, without much success. Somehow he landed in Erfurt, Thuringia, not far from Weimar.

He was good-looking, tall, wiry; he knew how to dress well with modest means, and there was a touch of Prussian upper-class arrogance in his manner. Here and there, for instance in Heidelberg, he had already played the part of a scion from an aristocratic family who happened to be in momentary financial difficulties. It had worked, he got 'loans', and now, in Erfurt, he decided to go the whole hog. He registered as 'Baron Korff' at the best hotel, and made a telephone call to the Potsdam residence of one of the ex-Kaiser's sons. Fortunately for Domela, the Prince was not available. But the trick was completely successful. It started among the hotel staff a train of conjecture which made 'Baron Korff' in no time His Imperial and Royal Highness Prince Wilhelm of Hohenzollern, eldest son of the Crown Prince and grandson of the Kaiser, honouring the loyal citizens of Erfurt with an incognito visit.

Republic or not, Erfurt, like the rest of Thuringia and most of

Prussia, was still full of pictures of the imperial family, and a large group photograph was hanging in the hotel manager's office. The noble guest did in fact bear some resemblance to Prince Wilhelm — both had fair hair, an oval face with prominent cheekbones, and they were about the same age. At once, Domela was addressed as Your Highness, in spite of his faint protests that he was just a simple baron; and soon, all Erfurt was licking his boots. There was, of course, no question of permitting him to pay any bills. Everybody was delighted to wine and dine him, to let him win at card games. No one could have been more surprised than Harry Domela himself at these manifestations of the German citizens' dream: to rub shoulders with a member of the former ruling family.

After a while he began to feel uneasy and tried to shake off his imperial shadow. It was impossible. The provincial snobs handed him round on a platter, passed him on to Gotha and Weimar where he was equally fêted. The local dignitaries, the businessmen, the hunting set — they were all scraping, bowing, clicking their heels before him; dowagers almost fainted with excitement when he deigned to address them. Even some Thuringian state ministers and a few *Reichswehr* officers turned up to shake his hand. Now he got really rattled. What if the Berlin press got hold of the story of the Prince's visit? Some reports and pictures had already appeared in the local papers.

He made a bold move. He presented himself to the regional *Reichswehr* commander and asked him to bring his influence to bear so that the newspapers in the area would stop writing about his 'private visit' to Thuringia; otherwise his 'family' would be embarrassed. Domela had instinctively assumed that in republican Germany the wishes of the military were still as good as commands, and he had been right. Not another word about him was published in the Thuringian press.

After a last glorious, drunken night in Weimar with a crowd of loyal 'subjects' — among them two unsuspecting police officers — he sneaked quietly to the railway station at dawn, bought a fourth-class ticket and took the slow train to Berlin, where he hoped to disappear in the throng. But when he arrived, bold headlines stared him in the face: 'FALSE HOHENZOLLERN PRINCE FOOLS DIEHARD MONARCHISTS,'

What had happened was that the Berlin editors had been sent some cuttings with photographs from Thuringian papers, published before the *Reichswehr* commander put a stop to it. Enquiries were made, and it was discovered that the real Prince Wilhelm had been nowhere near Erfurt or Weimar. Now all Berlin was enjoying the splendid hoax. The police were looking for him without knowing his real name; all they knew was that he resembled the ex-Kaiser's grandson. They found him as he was just about to cross the French frontier to enrol in the Foreign Legion.

Domela's trial was even more farcical than his exploits as the false Prince. Witness after witness declared that they had suffered no material loss through his pranks. On the contrary: hotel and restaurant managers said that the presence of 'His Highness' had increased their turnover considerably. Charity bazaars opened by him had collected record sums. Altogether, he had added much to the gaiety of life in dull Thuringia.

But many witnesses would have preferred not to be called — the duped aristocrats, the landowners and industrialists, the retired officers and town councillors who now looked rather foolish in the witness box. For the public gallery the trial was a highly amusing spectacle. The judge, wisely, gave Domela only a nominal short prison sentence.

Had Domela known what was now in store for him he would have given himself up much earlier instead of seeking oblivion in the Foreign Legion. There was an enormous Domela boom. He made a pile with his autobiography; he had to recreate his role on the stage and in a film.

The Hohenzollern family bore him no grudge. His 'mother', Crown Princess Cecilie, invited him for tea. 'A charming young man with very good manners,' was her verdict. 'You can't blame him for people's stupidity. There was just one thing that puzzled me: how on earth could they mistake him for our Wilhelm?'

Yet for many sincere republicans who were worried about the strength of Germany's reactionary forces the Domela affair had a different meaning. 'He has rendered us an invaluable service', wrote a widely-read political weekly in Berlin. 'No satire could have shown up better the ridiculousness of sycophancy, the true character of German monarchism.' Another journal suggested a scheme to 'recruit and train 500 Domelas, to be planted all over Germany in a well-planned action. Send them into the Foreign Ministry, the patriotic clubs, the veterans' associations – in short, wherever people are still longing to lick boots. Forward the 500 Domelas! They may help to create a new Germany.'

What happened to Harry Domela after his boom had died down has never been ascertained. One source said that he was sent to a concentration camp when the Nazis came to power and met his end there. But it seems more likely that he emigrated to South America where, for all we know, he may still be living.

I used to visit Munich in the early weeks of each year to enjoy the *Fasching,* the town's rapturous carnival season which Berlin has never known. In January, 1931, there was an extra treat in Munich: the trial of Franz Tausend, Ludendorff's goldmaker.

The ex-General had refrained from taking part in public life after his defeat as a presidential candidate. He and Mathilda, whom he had by now married, concentrated their efforts on their weekly journal dedicated to Nordic man, Germanic mysticism, and more revelations about Ludendorff's favourite subject, the Jewish–Catholic–Masonic conspiracy against Germany. He kept getting into debt with the printers and was in danger of being declared bankrupt. But a rescuing angel appeared just in time.

Franz Tausend was an analytical chemist without a job who claimed to have discovered a process for making gold from lead, potassium, mercury, sodium, and some 'secret ingredients'. Ludendorff, basically an uneducated man, fell for the age-old alchemistic spoof and agreed to lend his name, with all the weight it still carried among nationalist circles, to a society for the exploitation of Tausend's discovery – naturally for a share in the proceeds.

Again, as in the case of the man who claimed to power cars by water instead of petrol, a number of Germany's prominent industrialists invested money in Tausend's scheme; some came personally, others sent their experts, but all were taken in by his trick demonstrations, and bamboozled by the prestige of

Ludendorff, who talked about using the expected profits for 'patriotic purposes'.

With the invested money, Tausend established himself, his society, and his gold-making apparatus in a secluded mansion in the Bavarian forests. There was a steady stream of businessmen and emissaries from the industrial and financial world, whom Tausend admitted to some of his 'experiments': they would stare, fascinated, at the miracle-man's tweezers as he carefully fished out little golden globules from his bubbling crucible. Analysts found them to be genuine gold. Empty factories were secretly bought up in Frankfurt and Bremen for the mass production of the precious metal, to start as soon as the process was perfected. 'Gold vouchers', later to be exchanged for the real thing, were sold to investors. For nearly five years the incredible farce was running on.

Only one major backer grew suspicious as Tausend kept putting off the day when mass production could start, and informed the authorities. Investigations took the best part of two years, mainly because out of nearly five dozen victims only a few expressed doubts about Tausend's sincerity; the rest, among them men with some of the best-known names in Germany's economic sphere, were so frightened of being ridiculed as suckers at a public trial that they refused to charge him. Ludendorff, however, withdrew from Tausend's society before the trial – he had somehow got hold of much of the invested money and paid off his debts.

At the trial, which I attended, a police officer who had watched a 'gold-making' experiment revealed Tausend's secret: pretending to check his formulae, the swindler was holding a fountain pen, and the policeman saw a small gold pellet drop out of that pen into the crucible. Tausend went to prison for three years. 'One of the most charming of charlatans,' a Munich paper described him. 'After all, he did not rob any poor old-age pensioners or servant girls – he fleeced those who had amassed millions only a few years after the runaway inflation had cost most Germans their life savings. We have no pity for the big businessmen and bankers among the nationalists around General Ludendorff, who were cheated by Tausend.'

When he was released from prison, Hitler was in power. He tried his old scheme again, but the circles he approached had no need for a goldmaker now that their friends, the Nazis, were the masters of the Reich and of all the gold in the Reichs Bank vaults.

Sensational trials such as that of Tausend used to be reported in the German press by legal specialists who stuck rigidly to what the accused, the witnesses, the lawyers and the judges said, without describing the characters of a court-room drama or examining the personal and social problems involved. Now, most papers wanted to present human stories — not only from the court-room but from all walks of life. Writing for the press underwent a fundamental change; the trade of reporting turned into a literary art, and the readers were grateful for it.

The man who started this revolution in the German press was a Jewish journalist from Prague, Egon Erwin Kisch, whose name soon became the synonym for a new breed of newspapermen: impassioned, committed, with a sure instinct for the real problems and a sense of humour. Today we call the style Kisch created 'reporting in depth' — his own term was 'logical imagination', and he used it for writing on everything he saw, from the agony of a murderer's mother to a jolly home for Prague's ex-prostitutes, and from the down-and-out in Whitechapel to the fashion spies of Paris. We reporters all wanted to be Kischs; very few of us rose to his stature.

6

A CAPITAL OF THE ARTS

Looking back on the cultural life of the Weimar period one can only marvel at the wealth of achievements in so many spheres in such a short time, and practically only in one city, Berlin. Such a phenomenon does not, of course, appear out of the blue; none of the arts is an island, and its creative men and women need helpers and facilities. The miracle, which we were watching without being aware of its scope, was that it was all accumulating in our town: the theatres and the producers needed by the playwrights, the galleries and critics for the painters, the publishing companies for the writers, the opera houses and concert halls for the composers and conductors, the studios for the film directors and actors. It must have been a kind of chain-reaction, a snowballing process which brought about that concentration. 'Berlin's art and artists exerted a magnetic force,' wrote a colleague of mine. 'People came from all over the world to take part in the town's intellectual activities. It was a great happiness to be alive in those days.'

To do justice to those activities and achievements one would have to draw up a long, boring list of names and works, a catalogue of intellectual and artistic creations. I shall restrict my survey to those that impressed us young Berliners most, and mainly to the happenings of the years 1928 and 1929, the acme of the whole period.

In literature, it was not only the time when Kästner taught us to read poetry again; it was also that of the emergence of Erich Maria Remarque with the most exciting and controversial novel to appear in Germany between the two World Wars: *All Quiet on the Western Front*. Remarque was a sports reporter with Ullstein, Berlin's largest press corporation. He had served at the front as a teenager, and it had taken him ten years to digest the horrible experiences of a young soldier in the trenches; when he wrote them down he did so in brutal frankness, completely without the traditional heroic embellishment of German war literature. War is hell, was Remarque's simple message, and no patriotic cant can gloss over that truth.

Within three months, more than half a million copies were sold. The book swept Germany like wildfire. The chauvinists and nationalists hated it profoundly, for it debunked their cherished stab-in-the-back legend: The German soldier had not been betrayed by the 'November criminals' – he had, simply, had enough of the senseless slaughter. When the American-made film of the book opened in Berlin in 1930, Dr Goebbels sent his stormtroopers into the cinema, armed with stink bombs and white mice which they let loose, causing a panic among the audience. The authorities, instead of protecting the public against the Nazi mob, banned the film under the pretext that such demonstrations 'could harm Germany's image abroad'.

Other anti-war books by writers of Remarque's generation followed in the wake of *All Quiet;* publishers had been encouraged by Ullstein's fabulous success with a work that dared to attack the holy cow of Germany's national ideology. The right-wing writers did not have the talent to answer back with a convincing pro-war book, not even the most gifted among them, Hanns Johst, the former expressionist who had changed over to the Nazis (it was he who coined the famous phrase, 'When I hear the word *Kultur* I reach for my gun,' wrongly ascribed to Goering).

We were avid readers. Being able to talk about new books was a must; you had to buy, borrow or steal those everybody was discussing. Unfortunately, Germany never had a public library system like Britain.

What did we read? The first post-war years had witnessed the last but still powerful flares of expressionist literature – I remember the sensation caused by the outrageous title of Franz Werfel's 1919 novel, *Not the Murderer, the Murdered is Guilty.* Werfel was a Jew from Prague who, two decades later after his conversion to the Catholic faith, became internationally famous with his *Song of Bernadette,* the story of the miracle of Lourdes. Very popular in the early 1920s was Hermann Hesse with his spiritual guidance towards 'finding oneself' in this materialistic age. We read Lion Feuchtwanger, who came from Munich like myself.

His most popular biographical novels were the *The Ugly Duchess* and *Jew Süss*; he also wrote a brilliant *roman à clef* about the 1923 Hitler putsch, *Erfolg* (Success). The brothers Mann, Thomas the chronicler of the dying bourgeoisie and Heinrich the left-wing radical, were now at the height of their creative powers; Thomas, whose *Buddenbrooks* and *Magic Mountain* were the most widely translated modern German novels, got the Nobel Prize for Literature in 1929.

Arnold and Stefan Zweig, too, were widely believed to be brothers, but they had neither parents nor much else in common. The Socialist Arnold Zweig, from Silesia, moved us deeply with his war novel *The Case of Sergeant Grischa,* about the fight for justice for a wrongly condemned soldier; Stefan, from Vienna's upper class, enchanted us with his sensitive interpretations of men and women from history. His last great work, the autobiographical, nostalgic *World of Yesterday,* reached his surviving devotees only after he had killed himself in exile in 1942.

Franz Kafka, the German-language writer from Prague, remained completely unknown during his lifetime, but his impact after his death in 1924 was enormous. He had jotted down his private nightmares for himself, not for others to read, and asked his friend and fellow-writer Max Brod never to publish them. Fortunately, Brod disobeyed Kafka's wish but passed on to us his uncanny evocations of our innermost world of dreams and anxieties. Kafka was first published in Berlin.

The Berlin publishers were not all businessmen in a commercialised trade. Many were enthusiasts who considered it their duty to preserve the old literary values and encourage new talent. The most prominent of them was Samuel Fischer, whose list of authors included the brothers Mann, Gerhart Hauptmann, Stefan Zweig, Hermann Hesse, Carl Zuckmayer, the subtle Viennese writer Hugo von Hofmannsthal (librettist of *Der Rosenkavalier* and author of *Everyman,* the standard piece of the annual Salzburg Festival), and Alfred Döblin, the working-class doctor whose *Berlin-Alexanderplatz* was one of the few great novels set among the underprivileged people of our town.

As if our German literary production had not been enough to quench our thirst for reading matter, our hunger for food for thought, the twenties and early thirties were a great time for translated novels, mainly from the new Russian and American literatures. To those of us who believed in the future of Socialism, the early Soviet writers seemed to bring a whiff of fresh air into stuffy old Central Europe; that was the period of Lenin's 'New Economic Policy' when literature was liberalized and the Russians were again allowed to have their traditional sense of humour. The Berlin publishers who had the new Soviet writers translated opened for them the first important gate to appreciation in Europe.

The American authors published in Berlin also found a most perceptive readership, though for different reasons. Berlin had a great yen for America and Americanism, somewhat misunderstood as a superior, youthful civilization with a quickened pulse of life. Charleston and fast cars, the automatised eating-place 'Quick' on the Kurfürstendamm, the first European tabloid paper *Tempo* – it was all symptomatic of the Berliners' longing to be as American as the Americans. Upton Sinclair, John dos Passos, Hemingway and Sinclair Lewis were even more popular than their British and French contemporaries whose old, firmly established cultures had always been admired and envied by Germany's intellectuals.

It may seem an illogical attitude in a people that was now giving such powerful cultural impulses to the outside world. We should have been proud of it, but we were not as proud as we should have been. One reason, I think, was a subconscious doubt whether German culture was in fact up to international standards; it was an odd notion of inferiority. We were cheered by our cultural links with the outside world. For we knew that Berlin was not Germany, that our town was an oasis of artistic and intellectual creativity, surrounded by a cultural desert.

Yet there was also, ever present, a feeling of guilt: was not culture a nonessential luxury, ought we not to have occupied ourselves rather with serious matters such as the rise of unemployment and the dangers it might bring nearer for the whole society we were living in?

The theatres showed this split into entertainment and uneasiness quite clearly. Berlin had thirty of them, a great number considering that only a few hundred thousand inhabitants were potential customers. The rest would never go to a theatre or could not afford it. A handful of theatres, among them three opera houses, were run by the state or municipality, and another handful had music-hall or leg-show programmes. But many of the rest were run by groups who felt the moral or political obligation to produce *Zeittheater,* 'theatre of the times', meaning drama on topical problems. There was no lack of playwrights to provide the material: Bertolt Brecht, Ernst Toller, Georg Kaiser, Franz Werfel were foremost among those who shunned the 'escapist' theatre. To be sure, some of the lesser talents of the *Zeittheater* bored us stiff with their pep plays, their moralizing, their dialectical explanations why the world was bad and unjust – but didn't we feel virtuous after such an instructive evening in the stalls?

To tell the truth, the great productions of the entertainment theatre were much more exciting. They were the brilliant work of producers who made Berlin's stage of the late twenties the best in Europe. In the words of Bruno Walter, the conductor: 'The accomplishments of the Berlin theatre could hardly have been surpassed in talent, vitality, loftiness of intention, and variety.'

The outstanding personality was Max Reinhardt who, at the peak of his career, ran five Berlin theatres at the same time, plus one or two in Vienna. He was called the master of a new 'magical impressionism', of 'poetic realism', which killed the turn-of-the-century naturalist style on the stage stone dead. He was a Jew from Austria who had started as an actor but turned, at thirty, to production; at fifty, in the early 1920s, he had firmly established a new era in the theatre. All over Europe, and wherever there were theatres in America, producers were strongly influenced by his style, his way of bringing actors and audience into close communication however large the theatre was, his crowd management, his use of the apron stage. The first Reinhardt production I saw was his *Midsummer Night's Dream* in the Grosses Schauspielhaus, a former mammoth circus with seats for an audience of five thousand. It was pure witchcraft how he drew us all into the Shakespearean fairyland.

He knew very well what he was doing and why. 'I believe in the immortality of the theatre,' he said once. 'It is the blessed secret recess for those who have tucked their childhood away and want to keep playing with it to the end of their lives.' Reinhardt gave us the stuff dreams are made on; whatever he touched turned into pure theatrical gold, Shakespeare or Gerhart Hauptmann, the Greek tragedies or Molière, Shaw or Schiller, Galsworthy or Goethe – everything became a festival play in his hands. It was the very opposite of the 'alienation' which Brecht demanded, at least in his theoretical writings; yet Brecht was Reinhardt's *Dramaturg* for a few years, and no doubt learnt a lot from him for his own later work as a producer.

One of Reinhardt's great productions can still be seen (a posthumous reward which is granted to few artists of the theatre): Hofmannsthal's *Everyman,* with which Reinhardt inaugurated the Salzburg Festival in 1920. It is still staged in Reinhardt's original production every year, with the cathedral as its backdrop.

Even Erwin Piscator, the pioneer producer of the class-committed 'proletarian' stage and as such a soulmate of Brecht, admired Reinhardt while calling him 'a genius of theatrical wastefulness'. For Piscator, twenty years younger than Reinhardt, the stage was a political propaganda weapon of the working classes (though he came from a middle-class family of Protestant academics). His model was the revolutionary Russian theatre which brought the ideas and requirements of the new Soviet establishment to a largely illiterate rustic population. At first, Piscator expected to attract the Berliners to his proletarian theatre in the bare dance halls he had hired for his productions; but Berliners were neither rustic nor illiterate, and the German working class had never been interested in the theatre. So Piscator's early efforts were failures.

Only from 1927 onwards, when he worked in his own playhouse in Berlin's Westend, were his formidable talents widely recognized – by the bourgeois public. He premiered new plays by Toller, Brecht, and the radical left-wing doctor and dramatist, Friedrich Wolf; he produced the stage adaptation of Jaroslav Hašek's *Good Soldier Schweik* with the brilliant Czechoslovak comedian Max Pallenberg in the title role. He made George Grosz and John Heartfield design the sets: austere but effective, or 'constructivist' as he called them.

Piscator's productions were full of sarcastic wit and political satire; typical, for instance, was his idea of giving the villain in Schiller's youthfully rebellious *Robbers* the mask of Trotsky. Altogether, Piscator was our indispensable producer because he entertained us *and* made us feel virtuous by making us think about the social and political problems of our time.

The *Intendant,* or general manager, of the Berlin state theatres was Leopold Jessner, himself an outstanding producer who had a long-lasting influence on the modern theatre with one basic idea — steps. It started with his first Berlin production of Schiller's evergreen, *Wilhelm Tell.* When the curtain rose, even the most seasoned fans of the expressionist theatre were startled: the stage was almost entirely filled by one enormous, pyramid-like flight of stairs. All the action took place on these steps which the actors had to climb up and down, on which they stood or sat, and from which they rolled down when they were 'killed'. Also, Jessner had slanted the play into a formidable attack on tyranny, German-style, by dressing the hateful Gessler in a medal-studded general's uniform, by cutting proverbial dialogue lines about the fatherland, and so on. There was a full-scale scandal on the opening night, with yelling, whistling, stamping by right-wing theatregoers who got the message. The curtain had to be rung down several times, and actors shouted unscripted invectives at the demonstrators who, however, were in the end silenced by thunderous applause.

Originally, Jessner had wanted to convey the image of a Swiss mountain with his steps; but the effect was so overwhelming that he kept them as the hallmark of most of his subsequent productions. Some critics hailed them as modern abstract art on the stage, freeing the theatre of the conventional 'representational' scenery.

Theatre scandals which heralded successes delighted us in those years. Carl Sternheim's pre-war plays, scourging Wilhelminian society, had outraged the targets of his satire; his last ones, in the 1920s, were still sharp enough to provoke minor scandals. But a really splendid one occurred at the first night of young Carl Zuckmayer's comedy, *Der fröhliche Weinberg,* the 'Merry Vineyard'. Zuckmayer, who had grown up amidst the vines of the Rhine, fulfilled our hope that at least one new playwright would come up with a truly comic piece — humour had always been rare in German literature. However, Zuckmayer's broad comedy, set in the village scene he knew from his youth, was too much for a certain sector of the audience, and when his hero stepped out of the bushes buttoning up his fly the storm broke. But the play established Zuckmayer's fame. His best play of the Weimar era was *The Captain of Köpenick*, the dramatization of that immortal incident of Wilhelminian days when an old cobbler only had to put on an officer's uniform to make everybody obey him – including a platoon of soldiers whom he used to get the money from the municipal treasury at Köpenick. After World War II, Zuckmayer gained international recognition by his play *The Devil's General*, also based on a real-life figure, a *Luftwaffe* ace who opposed Hitler.

German acting had never been admired for its excellence; our foreign visitors, especially from England, thought there was too much shouting, hamming, and gesticulating on the Berlin stage. Still, we loved our actors and actresses, though the theatres often made the mistake of casting too many stars in one play – with the result that they tried to act one another off the footlights. Today, and outside Germany, those star names mean nothing, except in a few cases where exiled actors managed to get into English-speaking films: Elisabeth Bergner, Peter Lorre, Conrad Veidt, Lucie Mannheim. They had a hard time abroad after 1933. One of our greatest actors, old Albert Bassermann, succeeded in getting a screen test in Hollywood; the story goes that the film mogul who saw it took his cigar out of his mouth in astonishment and said, 'That guy got talent!' The result was a couple of minute parts.

It was very much different on the musical scene. In Weimar days, Germany had a wealth of great composers, conductors, soloists, singers, and orchestras, most of them working in Berlin unless on tour somewhere in the world. Otto Klemperer and Erich Kleiber were the chief conductors at the two state opera houses, Bruno Walter at the Municipal Opera; Wilhelm Furtwängler conducted the Philharmonic Orchestra, Arthur Schönberg (who completed his twelve-tone system in 1924) taught at the Prussian Academy of Fine Arts, Paul Hindemith at the Academy of Music. Richard Strauss' new operas had, as a rule, their first nights in the provinces, but were immediately afterwards produced in Berlin. Alban Berg's *Wozzeck* had its première under Kleiber's baton.

We had some six hundred concerts a year in Berlin; the highest-paid soloists were Fritz Kreisler, Arthur Schnabel and

Richard Tauber. Franz Lehár's, the Austrian composer's, operettas were first produced in Berlin, usually with Tauber and the legendary Fritzi Massary in the leading parts (Lehár's *The Merry Widow* was Hitler's favourite operetta).

As a jazz fan I went to the first night of a work which promised to be an unusual treat – a jazz opera by an unknown young composer from Vienna by the Czech name of Ernst Křenek. His inspiration, he said, had come from Paul Whiteman who had been on tour in Berlin with Gershwin's *Rhapsody in Blue*, and from Duke Ellington's 'Chocolate Kiddies', which had treated the Berliners to their first whiff of true negro jazz. Křenek's opera was called *Jonny spielt auf*, 'Johnny strikes up', and the hero was an American black as visualized by the composer, who had written his own libretto. His naive message was that jazz will conquer the world and turn it into a place where people love one another.

The last act was set in a railway station where Johnny's train is just about to leave. He jumps on the station clock and plays his violin while riding down the minute hand. 'A new world,' sings the chorus, 'is dancing across the oceans to take over Europe!' Křenek had meant well, but his Central European jazz was not the genuine article, and Johnny's *leitmotiv* was just a modernized 'Swanee River'. Still, it was all a great event, just the sort of thing we loved in Berlin.

'We were rather worried about the play, right until the end of the dress rehearsal. Personally, I was afraid the first night would be a complete flop, and I made arrangements to put on *Charlie's Aunt* at short notice if this one had to close down,' said the *Dramaturg* of the Theater am Schiffbauerdamm in Berlin when I interviewed him about the sensational success of the *Threepenny Opera* in the late summer of 1928.

There was no other theatrical event of the Weimar period which was as significant and at the same time as surprising as the triumph of the *Threepenny Opera*. It captured our mood and evoked our emotional response quite irresistibly. And not just in Berlin; all German-speaking Central Europe fell for the play so much that it became, within the short period before the Nazi regime banned it, the most widely-produced one, shown in approximately two hundred theatres – a record.

Its success was astonishing because, when analysed objectively, it is rather a hotchpotch of unrelated basic elements. Brecht had John Gay's *Beggars' Opera* — then exactly two hundred years old — translated by his collaborator and girl friend, Elisabeth Hauptmann. Then he went to work on the text, adapting it freely while keeping the principal characters and the place, London. He set the play, however, in an indetermined period. This timelessness permitted him to use many means and techniques of the modern theatre, from the musical to social drama, from literary parody to the cabaret song — all in the tense and transparent style he had developed in his own earlier plays and his poetry.

Brecht's intention seemed clear to us; he wanted to show up a social system in which the poor can be used for commercial gain, and in which a robber is no more of a villain that an entrepreneur. Yet there was no moralizing, no panacea for society's ailments: 'Man is good, the world is bad' — a simple philosophy with a touch of dialectical materialism *à la* Karl Marx, but as Brecht presented it, it was great entertainment. He gave his audience what they wanted most in the theatre: a dreamlike happy ending which was almost a satire on Marxist thinking; the anti-hero Macheath, about to be hanged, is saved by a royal messenger — he is not only set free but gets the gift of a castle and a pension for life. 'How easy and peaceful would be our lives,' says Mrs Peachum, 'if the royal messengers always came on time!'

The lyrics, which we were enthusiastically singing and quoting, were even more of a mixture. Some of the songs (the English word was from then on adopted in our everyday language) were inserted into the play as set pieces without much connection with the action; they had probably been written by Brecht before he even began to write the play: the 'Pirate Jenny' for instance, the song of the poor scullery maid in a shady seaside hotel, who fancies herself as the invading buccaneers' moll, taking bloody revenge on her betters who were ordering her about; or the 'Barbara Song', which appealed most of all to us young Berliners: about the girl who spurns her well-to-do, well-mannered, and spruce suitors but gives herself to the rough, unwashed he-man who sweeps her off her feet.

Brecht had one song, the 'Cannon Song' (about two cronies

127

from the British army in India), adapted from a Kipling poem, without acknowledgment. But the worst theft he committed was spotted by Berlin's most influential drama critic, Alfred Kerr. In a devastating review — he called the play 'rubbish', 'junk', and 'irrelevant' — Kerr disclosed that Brecht had lifted, also without any acknowledgment, the lyrics of no fewer than six songs in the *Threepenny Opera* from a German translation of François Villon's *Grand Testament*, published in 1911 by K. L. Ammer (who turned out to be an Austrian lieutenant and spare-time poet called Klammer). Brecht did not deny it at all, but 'explained' his piracy, unblushingly, with his 'deliberate laxity in matters of intellectual property', a phrase which became something of a classic quote in Germany. Yet unintentionally, Brecht had made Villon popular: thanks to him, we rediscovered France's greatest poet, that rebellious genius who wrote in our modern idiom five hundred years ago.

It had been Brecht's marvellous achievement to blend all these diverse elements into one whole work of art, with a fundamental message: *'Erst kommt das Fressen, dann kommt die Moral'* — 'First give us grub, and morals afterwards'. Still, the *Threepenny Opera* might have been only a short-lived success without Kurt Weill's 'magnificently simple' music, as Kerr called it. Weill, two years younger than Brecht, had studied under Hindemith; the two met first in the *Novembergruppe,* a circle of 'revolutionaries of the spirit' who pledged themselves in 1918 to work together in a new cultural era. Yet only Brecht and Weill teamed up and inspired each other.

For the *Threepenny Opera* Weill created an ideally complementary music, producing an artistic unity which made the play last throughout the best part of our century. What Kerr called 'magnificently simple' was rather deceptively simple; Weill caught the spirit of the play by creating tunes and rhythms for its unsophisticated characters, with slightly out-of-focus harmonies which suddenly dissolve into warm chords that touch the heart. There was much influence from jazz and Stravinsky in Weill's music, and he too 'stole' from another source — Peachum's mock-pious 'morning chorale', which Weill lifted straight from the original score of the *Beggars' Opera*. His 'orchestra' was Berlin's best jazz band, the Weintraub Syncopators.

Of the entire first-night cast of the *Threepenny Opera,* only one member rose to international fame: Weill's wife, Lotte Lenya, who played the part of Jenny. Because of her, the performance was nearly stopped; by an oversight, her name had been left out of the cast list in the programme, and when Weill found out halfway through the evening he demanded that the curtain should be rung down. Brecht placated him. When Hitler came to power, Weill and his wife emigrated to America, where he died in 1950, only fifty years old. Lotte Lenya survived as the ideal interpreter of his *Threepenny Opera* songs.

At the time of the play's first run I lived next door to Brecht's flat in West Berlin. I asked him for an interview to hear what he was planning to write next. 'Only what will be of use to the Communist Party,' he said sternly. In fact, he now began to write his *Lehrstücke,* short didactic playlets on the subject of Marxist revolution − cold, even brutal, and indigestible. Nor did *Mahagonny,* the next Brecht-Weill effort (premiered in 1930), remotely approach the success of the *Threepenny Opera.* It was only in exile after 1933 that he wrote his other full-scale works: *Mother Courage, Galileo, The Good Woman of Setzuan, Arturo Ui, The Caucasian Chalk Circle.* He returned to Communist East Berlin after the war and established himself as an outstanding producer of his own plays with the *Berliner Ensemble,* led by his actress wife, Helene Weigel. He died in 1956.

Kurt Weill was not a political man and certainly no Marxist. But his main rival in Berlin, Hanns Eisler, was, and the radical Left hailed him as their very own composer. I went to some of his lectures on composing at the 'Marxist Workers' College' to hear what ideas he had to offer. Melody and harmony, he said, were irrelevant; what mattered was rhythm, the marching rhythm of the proletariat. No wonder that few Eisler songs have survived.

Poster design for the *Threepenny Opera*
by Karl von Appen (1928)

129

Christopher Isherwood's diary of his impressions during the last years of the Weimar Republic, *Goodbye to Berlin,* aroused little attention when it appeared in 1939. He had been a 'furnished gentleman' in the flat of one of those innumerable Berlin landladies who had 'seen better days'. But after the war it underwent a remarkable metamorphosis: an American playwright dramatized it; then this play was made into a film; later it was reshaped as a musical; and the musical was turned into yet another film, *Cabaret.* It was a great success though it did not offer much enlightenment on everyday life in pre-Hitler Berlin, far removed as it was from Isherwood's perceptive and witty account of an era. There was just a grain of truth in it – the setting. For the cabaret was an important feature of Berlin's cultural life in those days, although the Anglo-American term means a rather different kind of entertainment.

What we called *Kabarett* was no leg-show, nor did it have elaborate decors, costumes, or an orchestra. As a rule, it was a small hall turned into a mini-theatre, often a former café, restaurant, or basement night-spot fitted with a bare podium and one or perhaps two pianos. The audience sat at tables, eating and drinking and watching the show. It consisted of songs and short

Joachim Ringelnatz, ex-sailor and poet, made his debut on the *Simplicissimus* stage in Munich and became later one of the best-known performers in the Berlin cabarets. He recited his Rabelaisian poems, often wearing a sailor's suit, and always drunk

scenes, solo and *ensemble* 'numbers'; there were rarely more than half a dozen people in the cast.

This may not sound very fascinating, compared to the entertainment value of Berlin's full-scale theatres; yet these cabarets – Berlin had usually about twenty or thirty of them – were great attractions for all those with intellectual and political interests. We called them 'literary' cabarets because their most important element were the words of the songs and scenes. Programmes changed every few weeks and offered comments on everything that concerned us: topical events, political trends, people in the limelight, ridiculous or worrying features of public life, all seen from a more or less leftist angle – there was not enough sense of humour on the Right to feed a cabaret. Satire, parody, hard-hitting or good-natured wit were the styles of the literary cabaret in lyrics and dialogue, often contributed by well-known writers like Walter Mehring, Brecht, Tucholsky and Kästner; many cabarets also had their resident authors. Sometimes cabaretists sang or spoke their own texts.

There were quite a number of splendid performers with that characteristic talent the cabaret demanded; actors or singers used to the big stage were usually no good. You had to believe in what you were saying or singing, you had to scorn or hate what you were attacking, and feel sympathy for the causes you stood up for in your texts. For the most outstanding cabaretists their appearance before an audience was not just a performer's turn but a means of winning friends and influencing people.

I came to know the cabaret scene quite well. I had discovered that I could write reasonably good lyrics for topical songs; to some extent this was a 'bespoke' job as each cabaret artist needed a special type of text. But it was rather a spare-time hobby than a remunerative occupation; the fees which performers, writers and musicians could earn by working for a small cabaret were negligible, yet one was proud to have one's name printed in the programme. It was also gratifying to carry on an old European tradition: the cabaret was born in France in the middle of the eighteenth century when poets sang their anti-royalist *chansons* and sarcastic ditties in the taverns, and in the nineteenth it developed into a medium for criticism and opposition first in the Austro-Hungarian monarchy and then, around the turn of the century, in Germany, starting in Munich.

131

Some cabarets of the 1920s specialized in sex and nudity. They had their own journal, called *Love*

The momentous time of Berlin's literary cabarets came in the 1920s. Although censorship had all but gone and we could express our political opinions and criticisms in print, a cabaret could say much more, and sharper and wittier, than any editor would publish in his journal. Scandals were almost the daily bread of the cabaret; insulting the audience was an accepted routine, but sometimes the artists were insulted – in the 'Cabaret of the Nameless' for instance, so called because it offered anybody a chance to mount the podium, perform, and be hooted down. Then there was the 'Cabaret of the Impossibles' whose programmes were truly outrageous, and where performances often culminated in brawls.

We regarded our cabarets as political weapons in the fight against the Nazis, the generals, the *Junkers,* and our hypocritical or cowardly ministers; audiences were, of course, small, but points from songs and jokes from scenes went the round all over the town.

The most famous and certainly the most courageous of cabaretists was Werner Finck, a tall, bespectacled young man with a slight stoop and a shy smile who started his cabaret, the *Katakombe,* in the autumn of 1929. Within a few weeks, it was almost a symbol of intellectual resistance against the rising tide of Nazism and reaction. Finck, as the compere of his show, had a unique knack of establishing at once an intimate, knowing relationship with his audience; he never finished his sentences, yet we all understood what he was getting at. He wrote most of the texts himself. I remember a typical scene, the examination of a somewhat dense law student; the professor wants to get him to talk about diminished responsibility:

> *Professor.* Now you read the papers, and every day there are reports about defendants being acquitted by the judge though their crimes are proven. They are acquitted not because they are minors or have acted in self-defence, but because – what? *Student* (with brightening face). Because they are Nazis, Herr Professor!

Stormtroopers used to come to the *Katakombe* and heckle Finck. Once they shouted at him, 'Jewboy!' He smiled disarmingly: 'You are mistaken. I only look so intelligent.'

His cabaret managed to hang on until 1935. Werner Finck took incredible risks. One day the Gestapo arrested the whole cast, and he was sent to a concentration camp. He was eventually released after signing the customary undertaking not to

Werner Finck,
caricatured by himself

complain about his treatment. He was asked by his friends what the food had been like in the camp. He replied, carefully: 'Like in a respectable family who, through no fault of their own, have got into rather straitened circumstances.' This became a classic Finck quotation in Berlin.

He was eventually drafted into Hitler's army, but he survived. Many other cabaretists did not. As outspoken critics of the Nazis, or simply as Jews, they were on their black lists, and that meant death. Some killed themselves; others got out of Nazi Germany while they still could. But wherever they found refuge, groups of them started cabarets in exile. I was among such a group – actors, singers, writers, musicians, stage designers – who came together to London shortly before the outbreak of World War II, and it was for us a matter of course to put on a cabaret show. Among London's theatregoers this new kind of entertainment was a great success, but after two weeks' run in a small West End theatre we finished up with a thumping deficit.

Already before the first World War, Max Reinhardt had been building up a more elaborate type of cabaret, the *Kabarett-Revue,* roughly equivalent to Herbert Farjeon's 'little revue' in London. It required a proper though intimate theatre, actors and actresses who could sing rather than cabaretists, and a resident writer-composer team. In the mid-twenties, the lyricist Marcellus Schiffer – who had written two opera libretti for Hindemith – and the popular composer Mischa Spoliansky created their own brand of cabaret-revue; each new prodution was an event we eagerly looked forward to, and we were never disappointed. Here was the very essence of Berlin's sharp, smart, mischievous yet basically affectionate wit. These revues were always topical though they lacked the political aggression of the small cabarets; they satirized the foibles and fashions, absurdities and eccentricities of the times in a shrewd and breezy way. Margo Lion, the Franco-German wife of Marcellus Schiffer, tall and irresistibly funny in her caricatures of the 'modern' female snob, was usually in the lead; she was joined by a talented newcomer with perfect legs and a husky voice by the name of Marlene Dietrich. In 1928, at 24 years of age, she began to do solo turns in the Schiffer-Spoliansky revues, and the critics wrote about her 'inimitable mixture of elegance and vulgar smartness'.

Friedrich Hollaender
(from a press cartoon
in the Berlin
tabloid paper *Tempo*)

Friedrich Hollaender had always been his own one-man team of writer and composer, born as he was (in London, by the way) into a family of writers and composers. His serious musical studies with the original Engelbert Humperdinck, the composer of *Hänsel and Gretel,* helped him to develop a solid craftsmanship; he was also the best accompanist on the piano his interpreters could have wished for. The slight little man with the large doe eyes and the wrinkled face started his career in Reinhardt's cabaret-revue in 1920; ten years later, after contributing to nearly all the literary cabarets that sprang up in Berlin, he opened his own revue theatre in the Westend.

Hollaender aimed at a high political and ideological standard of the cabaret, which he regarded as 'a battlefield where the clean weapons of sharpened words and loaded music can beat those of murderous steel'. Yet his superb talents as an entertainer got the better of him; there was little aggression in his revues but a great deal of brilliant topical satire. Still, a few outstanding political numbers impressed an audience that had come for sheer amusement, such as – in *Allez hopp,* a revue with circus life as its setting – the scene in which a tight-rope walker balances between the spectre of mass unemployment and the abyss of dictatorship.

On the opening night of his revue theatre, Marlene Dietrich was spotted among the audience. She was carried bodily to Hollaender at his piano, and both were made to do a new song of his that was now conquering Berlin, 'Falling in love again', from the film *The Blue Angel.*

The German film industry had made great strides since the *Caligari* days. The silent screen had been developed to an artistic medium in its own right, not just an entertainment with one dimension missing. True, Ernst Lubitsch had deserted us; after making his name known internationally with his historical and comedy films he emigrated to Hollywood in 1922. When he landed in the States and was asked what his plans were, he replied, 'The American public, with its mind of a twelve-year-old child, must have Life As It Ain't.'

But we had other directors who put the silent German film in the lead, most of them working in the UFA studios at Neubabelsberg, just outside Berlin. There was Fritz Lang, monocled and self-assured, who had studied painting and architecture in his native Vienna. He had his first decisive success with a thriller made when German inflation was at its height, *Dr Mabuse the Gambler.* His 'hero' was a villain with a mastermind on the brink of insanity; Lang created great tension by using extraordinary camera angles and cutting techniques. His next production was *The Nibelungs,* that medieval Teutonic tale of murder, treasure and treachery. He left his audience gasping at enormous mountain castles, forests with gigantic trees, vast halls that dwarfed Cecil de Mille's expensive Hollywood sets. How was it done? A German engineer by the name of Schüfftan had invented an ingenious system of combining life-size scenery with reflected miniature pictures: the set was built to a height of only about three metres, high enough to give the actors freedom of movement; the entire upper part of the scene was painted on cardboard sheets, sometimes no larger than a postcard, and these were reflected into the lens by a mirror. Instead of painted pictures, small-scale models could also be used.

Schüfftan's system gave Fritz Lang's films the advantage that they could be made on comparatively small budgets yet

Above: The fantastic townscapes in Fritz Lang's *Metropolis* were not built life-size but reflected into the camera lens by Eugen Schüfftan's ingenious technique using miniature drawings and models. *Below*: A scene from Fritz Lang's *Dr Mabuse the Gambler*, set in a nightspot for the profiteers with its sexy, hedonistic atmosphere of the inflation period

137

impressed audiences all over the world by their apparently lavish sets. In *Metropolis,* made in 1926, he conjured up skyscraper scenes and giant machines for a science-fiction story which, however, suggested a rather naive solution for the controversy between capital and labour. But for his first sound film he used a real-life plot, the case of a demented mass murderer played by Peter Lorre; it was based on a series of child murders in the Rhineland. The film was most successful under its unusual title *M.* In fact, Lang's original title had been 'Murderers Amongst Us', but the prompt reaction to the announcement of this title was a furious protest by the Nazis who assumed that 'the Austrian Jew Lang' was making a film about them. The UFA, which had been bought up a year earlier by the nationalist news-paper and mining tycoon Alfred Hugenberg, decided to spare the tender feelings of the Nazis, and the film was called just *M.* Fritz Lang wrote later that this episode behind the UFA scenes made him 'come of age politically'; as he was discussing the re-titling issue with the production manager he happened to grip the man by his lapel – and felt the NSDAP badge fastened to the inside, out of sight, but ready to be pinned to the front as soon as the Nazis took over. Lang had stumbled upon a widespread German 'fashion' of the last years of the Weimar Republic.

Another great Austrian-born director who began his career in the silent era was Georg W. Pabst. His *Joyless Street* was remarkable for more than one reason. It was the first film about the human tragedy of inflation. The leading part was played by Asta Nielsen, the Danish-born actress who had been a German film star since the early 1900s; and Pabst had engaged another Scandinavian actress to play opposite her – Greta Garbo. It was her first role outside Sweden and her last one in Europe; her next port of call was Hollywood. *The Joyless Street* was based on a story by a Viennese Jewish author, Hugo Bettauer, who was shot dead at his desk before the film was screened. The murderer was a Nazi, who took revenge for another novel by Bettauer, a 'futuristic' fantasy which was destined to become an awful truth fifteen years later. It was set in Vienna and entitled *The City without Jews.*

Many film directors whose names and works became well known, especially after they moved to Hollywood, started their careers in the studios around Berlin. F. W. Murnau turned Bram Stoker's horror story *Dracula* into his *Nosferatu* in 1922; then he directed *The Last Laugh,* which had a courageous plot about an old hotel porter, played by Emil Jannings, who ends up as the 'last man' of the establishment, the lavatory assistant. Called to America, Murnau teamed up with Robert Flaherty for a joint production of the − still famous − South Sea film *Tabu.* He died soon afterwards.

On the whole, Berlin's film scene in the Weimar era got much of its impulses and original ideas from young 'immigrants' from Austria and points further east. Two of them, Robert Siodmak and Billy Wilder, captured the peculiar atmosphere of their host city, with its robust pleasures and erotic aura, its crowded lake beaches and romantic groves in a charming semi-documentary, *People On Sunday,* shot without professional actors. Yet another Austrian, Joseph von Sternberg, directed that classic of early sound films, *The Blue Angel,* based on Heinrich Mann's *Professor Unrat,* in 1930. It was the story of a school tyrant's downfall, set in the days of the Wilhelminian establishment; in this part, Emil Jannings was again excellent. But it was 'our indigenous Berlin vamp Marlene Dietrich who raised the film to its lasting importance. Sternberg shot it simultaneously also in an English-speaking version to overcome the language difficulties in foreign distribution: Lola was an English 'artiste' and the Professor a teacher of English to make their dialogue in that language plausible. That awkward version has still not disappeared from the world's screens which keep reviving the most famous of Germany's pre-Hitler sound films.

A Bulgarian director, Slatan Dudow, made the most outspoken political film of that period, *Kuhle Wampe*; that was the name of a Leftist weekend camp of Berlin's working-class youth. Brecht wrote the script; Dudow shaped it in the Russian style − Berlin audiences were thrilled by the Soviet films, starting with *Battleship Potemkin*; Hanns Eisler composed the music which gave the German Communist movement a new battle hymn, the rousing 'Song of Solidarity'. The film was promptly banned by the censor, but widely shown in working-class clubs.

But Pabst's *Kameradschaft* (Comradeship) of 1931 could not be touched by the censor, although it was also essentially a political film. Its theme was human understanding and mutual help across the frontiers. The setting, a coalmine which stretches across the Franco-German border, gave Pabst an opportunity for exploring new visual and acoustic techniques; through the tragedy of a mine disaster he drove home the message that ordinary people's decency and sympathy can surmount all national barriers. No wonder that this anti-chauvinistic film, like his anti-war picture *West Front 1918*, enraged the Nazis nearly as much as *All Quiet on the Western Front*.

An independent, non-commercial company produced an outstanding picture with an all-woman cast, directed by a woman director, Leontine Sagan, in 1931, after a successful play by a woman writer, Christa Winsloe: *Girls in Uniform*. It showed how much of the old Prussian officers' spirit was still alive in the Weimar Republic. The film was set in a Potsdam boarding-school for girls from aristocratic families, and its subject was the generation gap between the majority of teachers, still steeped in the imperial past, and the girls who were trying to adjust themselves to the new era: a conflict which ends in tragedy.

'The Jew is the evil spirit of decay. Whenever he smells filth and rot, he crawls out from his hideout and begins to corrupt everything . . . I hear you say: "But there are good Jews too." When you say that you admit that the rest of that race is basically rotten and despicable. . . . We are the Jews' enemies because we are Germans. The Jews are our great curse. But things will change as surely as we are Germans!'

Dr Goebbels, the little Rhinelander whom Hitler had appointed his propaganda chief, wrote this in his party paper *Angriff* (Attack) in 1928. The battle against Weimar culture had begun, and as a true provincial he hated all that made Berlin a cosmopolitan capital of the arts, of intellectual progress, of liberalism — that whole way of life which set the town apart from the rest of Germany. The most effective accusation in the Nazis' provincial campaigns was that Berlin's artistic life was largely run by Jews.

There was some truth in it. More than 200,000 Jews, over a third of the entire Jewish population of Germany, were living in

Berlin in the late 1920s, many of them newcomers from the provinces, from Austria and Eastern Europe. The liberal climate of the capital had attracted them, a climate in which their special talents and abilities found ample scope: an opportunity which, for historical and political reasons, they had never had before to such an extent.

Perhaps more than in other Central and Western European countries, the Jews had been the Cinderellas and scapegoats of their host society in Germany since the early Middle Ages. They had to live in ghettoes and were barred from taking part in the arts and crafts, in agriculture and other productive activities. Thus they were restricted to commerce and finance, and they proved to be very good at it. But whenever a ruler needed money, he squeezed it out of his Jews; and whenever the population grew dissatisfied with its condition, there were always the Jews who could be blamed for any calamities, from price rises to epidemics.

Persecuted, plundered, or thrown out of Germany by force, most Jewish communities went east and re-settled in Russia and Poland, but after a short period of respite persecution began there as well. Massacres by the savage Cossacks in the seventeenth century may have cost half a million Jews their lives. Slowly the survivors began to trickle back into Central Europe, where the 'Age of Enlightenment' culminated in the emancipation of the Jews, their — at least theoretical — acceptance as citizens with full rights early in the last century.

Still, commerce and finance remained their main fields of occupation; prejudice and protectionism kept them from taking up most other trades (there was, for instance, never a Jewish working-class in Germany). It took quite some time until Jewish fathers could send their boys to the universities to become doctors, lawyers, or scientists. This stage was reached little more than a century ago, and even then Germany's overwhelmingly chauvinistic and antisemitic students made life miserable for their Jewish fellows.

But the arts and other cultural activities were open to them without restrictions, and here the Jews showed talents which had been latent for two thousand years. Logically, the German people should have welcomed and encouraged the enhancement of their cultural life and international prestige by the achievements of their Jewish fellow-citizens; but nations do not react logically. It was still regarded as a blemish to be a Jew; those who liked and admired a Jewish writer, musician, painter, or actor never mentioned the fact; if it was mentioned this was done as an intentional denigration. 'Jewish art', 'Jewish culture' were antisemitic slogans.

Small wonder that the German Jews who were active in those spheres tried to gloss over their extraction or even hush it up. The philosophy of the great majority of German Jews was 'assimilation': Jewishness was supposed to be merely a matter of religion; and if they got themselves baptized (quite a number of Jews did), that should have been the end of their discrimination. Of course it was not. Some tried to be more German than the Germans. I remember from my school days in Munich a particularly chauvinistic history teacher with a Jewish name and face who liked to point out at every opportunity that he was a Protestant. We made our jokes about him and his masquerade. I wonder how he fared later, under the Nazis; to them, any attempt at assimilation, at absorption into the German population was a Jewish trick to facilitate the undermining of the German spirit.

Seen against that background to the Jewish 'problem' in the Weimar Republic, the phenomenon of Berlin was all the more remarkable. Here, thousands of Jewish artists, intellectuals and cultural workers of every kind had gathered to produce their best, and the result contributed to the elevation of the town to the European, if not international, capital of culture, though only for a few years. There is no doubt that Jewish talent, imagination, lightness of touch, sense of taste and — last not least — sense of humour were responsible for much of what we now call, in retrospect, Weimar culture. The sad proof of this came after 1945, when Berlin, like the whole of Germany, was in a deep cultural depression. There were no more Jews to help lift it up again, as they had done after that first lost war a quarter of a century earlier.

But to call Weimar culture 'Jewish culture' would be wrong. What we witnessed was a natural symbiosis of Jewish and non-Jewish German talents, inspiring, fertilizing, complementing each other. This was most obvious on a personal level where Jews and Gentiles either worked together or competed with each

142

other as professional colleagues: Brecht and Weill, Gropius and Mendelsohn, Pabst and Lang, Einstein and Planck, Kästner and Tucholsky, Reinhardt and Piscator, to mention but a few 'couples'. And this 'chemistry' of personalities was not confined to the younger generation with its strong creative drive; for instance, there were still the two grand old men of German impressionism, Max Slevogt and Max Liebermann, the Bavarian-born cosmopolitan and the plain-speaking Berlin Jew who once, asked whether he had time to paint Hindenburg again, replied disdainfully, 'Hindenburg? I can piss him in the snow.'

We were well aware that the arts were becoming a sector of the political battlefield, and those of us who had access to the mass media tried to help in the fight. Gradually, Berlin was changing into Europe's hot spot. We were more and more isolated, concerned with our struggles, and increasingly oblivious of what was going on in the outside world. We did read, of course, about the black day in Wall Street late in 1929, but what we felt about it was almost a kind of malicious glee, of *Schadenfreude* that big, rich America was now getting into the troubles of economic crisis and unemployment, which we knew only too well; but did all that concern us? We laughed over a joke that was making the rounds: 'I got a letter from my uncle in America,' a Berliner tells his friend. 'Oh, marvellous,' says the friend, 'what does he write?' 'He asks if I can send him ten dollars.'

Soon we were laughing on the other side of our faces.

7

THE LAST YEARS OF THE REPUBLIC

We had nearly lost sight of Hitler; he rarely came to Berlin. But he had not been wasting his time since his release from the fortress of Landsberg. His party had been in ruins after the failure of the putsch, and he needed money to build it up again. Smart as he was, he knew very well that the big money-bags would show him the door if he came to them himself, cap in hand; so he used his social acquaintances as go-betweens for whispering the right things in the right ears. There were a few Munich *salons* where he met influential aristocrats, diplomats, businessmen and senior officials, some of whom were prepared to act for him as middlemen. One of the first major industrialists with whom he got in touch in this way, and whom he roped in to finance the NSDAP as a defence force against the Communists and the trade unions, was Fritz Thyssen; he had inherited the largest steel works in the Ruhr from his father. Once Hitler had got him, contacts with other magnates followed easily. Within four or five years after Landsberg, the party had large sources of income.

Hitler spent most of the industrialists' money for the purpose for which it was given: the training and enlargement of his fighting force of SA (the stormtroopers) and SS (*Schutzstaffeln*, guard units). The SS, originally Hitler's bodyguard, were now turned into his shock troops; in 1929, the former Bavarian poultry farmer Heinrich Himmler was appointed their commander.

One of Hitler's new contacts, and eventually his most important, was Alfred Hugenberg. He had been Director General of Krupps, the armament corporation; after leaving it he established, like Stinnes, a large industrial and commercial empire of his own during the inflation – but he was shrewd enough to keep it together, constantly adding to it, in the following years. He was, in his way, a passionate patriot, interested in money merely as a means of power politics, and of acquiring the mass media for influencing public opinion. He bought up a very large group of newspapers, read by the disgruntled middle classes in Berlin and the provinces; he also owned the news agency that supplied them with copy, effectively slanted against the democratic system. In 1927 he took over the UFA, Germany's leading film company, turning it gradually into a dream factory of escapist *schmaltz* and heroic *kitsch*, such as romanticized patriotic pictures about Frederick the Great. Within a few years, the UFA was no longer part of Germany's eminence in the art of the film; we had to look to the smaller, independent companies for important productions.

Hugenberg was a short, fat man with a one-inch crop of grey hair like Hindenburg and a bushy white moustache twirled up like the Kaiser's. Everything about him was deliberately old-fashioned: the stand-up collar, the cut-away he was usually wearing, the golden watch chain spanning his belly. He probably regretted that his physique did not enable him to present a more martial image in keeping with his nationalist philosophy. He started his political career as a *Reichstag* member of the German National Party; soon he became its leader.

Hitler, the upstart, was hardly a man after the heart of this representative of the armament industry and high finance; Hugenberg intended to use him only as a helpmate in his struggle against the Weimar Republic. Nor did he trust the SA and SS as a fighting force for Germany's nationalist revival, his ultimate aim. So he backed another paramilitary organization, the *Stahlhelm* (steel helmet). This militia, recruited mostly from the right-wing middle-class, never grew very large, but it joined the SA in its street fights against the Communist and the Social-Democratic private armies.

These troubles in the streets of Berlin were still in their early phase when Hitler came to the capital in 1929 to speak at a mass meeting. As a journalist I thought I ought to have a closer look at the man who had seemed no more than a mountebank in his pre-putsch days in Munich, but whose recent successes as a speaker were undeniable. What was his personal attraction for certain sectors of the German public? He had been campaigning in the provinces for three years and got a few Nazi candidates elected in several *Länder* parliaments and even in the *Reichstag*.

The mass meeting I wanted to attend was in Berlin's largest hall, the Sportpalast; its most popular annual event was the Six-Day Bicycle Race. I don't know how many people it could accommodate, but it certainly offered a magnificent arena for any mammoth show. And this was exactly to what we were treated.

I say 'we' because I took my cousin along on the other of my two press tickets. She was to be my camouflage, so to speak: the perfect image of a German girl, with long golden hair and big blue eyes, while I did not look very much like an 'Aryan' prototype. Her curiosity about Hitler's magic formula of success, if he had one, was as great as mine.

As we entered the hall, some of that magic opened up before our eyes. The Nazi showmanship was as impressive as it was garish. From the entrance to the rostrum at the far end of the hall a double row of hundreds of stormtroopers formed a lane along a red carpet on which the *Führer* was to march in. Behind them, a sea of faces, most of them with hats, for the majority were women. The carpet lane was so long that its end was hardly discernible; we had no choice but to run that gauntlet past all those stormtroopers as the press table was right at the rostrum. So we advanced over the red carpet, she striding ahead, I slinking behind her. Perhaps our march took only a few minutes, but they felt endless. I hoped fervently that I would never again see so many uniformed Nazis in all my life.

At last we got to our seats. All around the vast hall, enormous swastika banners were hanging from the walls. A brass band was playing military marches. Suddenly the music stopped in mid-air; then it started again with the 'Badenweiler March', Hitler's favourite piece of music. The entrance doors opened wide, and there he was, a tiny figure seen at that distance. The crowd went wild, shouting '*Heil*', raising arms in the Nazi salute. As he marched nearer in his SA uniform and peaked cap, acknowledging the crowd's greeting with a half-raised forearm, I could not help feeling that this was a ham actor rather than a popular leader: that absurd little moustache (in fact a tradition among his fellow-countrymen in Upper Austria), that forced military gait, that self-important scowl — it all seemed somewhat phoney.

146

Behind him marched a group of his henchmen in brown and black uniforms; I recognized Röhm, podgy and flabby, and Himmler in full SS regalia but with the face of a dull, harsh teacher and with small, cold eyes behind the pince-nez. Only Goebbels wore a civilian suit; he was limping along energetically, trying to keep up with his master's stride. They all took their seats on the rostrum just above us.

Goebbels, as the Berlin *Gauleiter* and propaganda chief, started the evening's programme of speeches. At the end he 'introduced' the *Führer* with a flourish and an abundance of superlatives. Hitler rose, and again the crowd went wild. He commanded silence with an imperious gesture and began to speak.

He had learnt much since his early Munich time; the story we had heard, that he had taken lessons in elocution and rhetoric with a well-known retired actor in Munich, was obviously true. He had been trained to speak to a certain pattern. He had no script, only a small piece of paper apparently listing the subjects he wanted to cover. He spoke, as it were, in paragraphs, in passages of a few minutes' length, beginning each of them in a moderate tone, then rising in pitch and volume, and bellowing out the last words in an impassioned roar. This was always the signal for the crowd to burst into applause. He shot out his right hand, with lifted finger as though he had not yet finished his argument while, in fact, looking at the piece of paper in his left hand for the next subject. Then, when the applause had subsided, he began the next passage to exactly the same pattern.

I cannot remember much of what he said, except that he repeated his favourite slogans: about the ten years for which Germany had now been 'languishing in shame and dishonour', about the *Diktat* of Versailles that had enslaved the German people, about the hold which 'Jewish high finance' had over them, and about the 'Jewish *Kulturbolschewismus*', the disgrace of Berlin. There was, however, one new phrase which stuck in my mind because I nearly burst out laughing: 'Don't buy foreign lemons, eat German apples instead', or something to that effect.

It was all a primitive yet successful performance, and the repetitive rhythm seemed to produce a kind of hypnotic trance in the crowd. When they woke up at the end and made their way to the exit, we found ourselves amidst shining faces and dreamy eyes. These bemused, insecure people had been given a potent injection of faith in a leader and a movement that would put everything right.

While Berlin was at the height of its cultural glory, in October, 1929, two momentous events took place which hastened the end of the Weimar Republic. One was the Wall Street crash which we did not take seriously as it happened to other people in a faraway country; but the other concerned us immediately. It was Stresemann's death of a heart attack at the age of only fifty-one.

His disappearance from the German political scene was a grievous loss because there was no one to replace him. This son of a Berlin beer-shop owner, conscious of his humble origins throughout his life, had founded the right-of-centre German People's Party at the end of the war; yet he was a sincere believer in democracy, liberalism, and international understanding – in all the basic values of the Weimar system. He had, as Reichs Chancellor, assembled the team that brought inflation to an end; he had, as Foreign Minister, negotiated the Dawes and Young plans which reduced Germany's reparations to a tolerable level; he had prepared the Allied withdrawal from the Rhineland by the Locarno Pact, which was the first Franco-German agreement of friendly co-operation ever concluded between the two traditional enemies. He received the Nobel Peace Prize, awarded jointly to him and his French counterpart, Briand, in 1926. In that year, he guided Germany into the League of Nations as a full member. In short, his achievements in bringing Germany back into the family of nations showed up Hitler's lies about her still 'languishing in shame and dishonour'.

Had Stresemann lived, there might have been a chance of stopping the Nazi movement in its tracks. But the men who appeared in his place after his death were a sorry lot; each time yet another Chancellor or Foreign Minister was presented to us we were bewildered: how on earth could these nonentities, these blatantly self-interested reactionaries be expected to get us out of the difficulties which were now accumulating? That a few of them were downright traitors to the Republic became clear only when it was too late.

Things began to change rapidly. The Wall Street crash had not, after all, been just a flash in someone else's pan. When it happened, Germany had one and three quarter million unemployed, nearly half a million of them in Berlin; by January, 1930, two months or so later, the number for the whole Republic had already doubled. The great depression was now world-wide, and Germany seemed particularly vulnerable because of her lack of economic and political stability. Once more, a vicious circle was in operation, reminiscent of that of the inflation: exports dwindled quickly as all industrial nations were caught in the crisis, foreign investments in Germany stopped, and as a result factories and companies went bankrupt by their hundreds, throwing their workers and office staff out into the streets. The jobless, of course, could not afford to buy anything but the bare essentials of life; tax revenue dropped as the volume of trade and incomes shrank, yet more and more people needed social benefits.

These benefits were small, hardly enough to keep body and soul together; the Social Democrats and the Communists demanded increases, the *Zentrum* and the Right refused them. In March, 1930, the coalition government fell, and another one, with half a dozen parties represented in the cabinet, took over under a new Chancellor; but the Social Democrats, still the strongest party in the *Reichstag*, did not take part.

A *Zentrum* politician, Heinrich Brüning, was the new Chancellor, at 45 the youngest government leader Germany had ever had. He was a conservative Catholic, a mediocre speaker and a dour man without many social graces. With his bland face, bald pate, and rimless glasses he might have been a priest. He had studied economics and was no doubt full of good intentions, but lacked the gift of putting them into practice. Unable to swing the *Reichstag* members to his side and make them accept his deflationary crisis recipe of higher taxes and lower government expenditure, he resorted to what looked very much like a panic measure: he invoked Article 48 of the Weimar Constitution, declaring a state of emergency.

From now on, Germany was to be ruled by presidential decrees. He had no difficulty in getting old Hindenburg to sign anything he wanted enacted. There was a bitter joke in Berlin: at an audience with the President, a politician put his sandwich wrapping-paper on the table by mistake, whereupon Hindenburg's aide whispered anxiously, 'Take that away, for heaven's sake, or he'll sign it!'

The first thing Brüning decreed, among furious protests inside and outside the *Reichstag*, was to dissolve it; new elections were fixed for September, 1930. The election campaign started immediately, not only with unwonted intensity, but with a new dimension: the political turmoil boiled over into the streets.

It was a miniature civil war that was going on during those last years of the Republic. In Berlin it became a regular feature of the town's night life. It was fought by five groups; two of them were the most murderous of the lot – the SA and the Communist *Roter Frontkämpfer-Bund* (Red Front Fighters' League), *Rotfront* for short. These two were implacable enemies engaged in a more or less organized guerilla warfare mainly in the working-class districts; firearms were occasionally used, casualties – dead and seriously wounded – were frequent. When we read the newspaper reports about these street battles we sometimes had the impression that Germany was fast approaching the crossroads of her destiny, and that the alternatives were a Nazi dictatorship or a Communist one.

But there were two further groups of fighters, one on the right and one on the left. The nationalists had their *Stahlhelm,* backed directly by industrial circles; the Social Democrats had their *Reichsbanner,* organized as a movement for the defence of the republican establishment, but in practice mostly engaged in doing battle with the stormtroopers. Yet they never joined forces with the Communists – the two leftist groups were at great pains to keep apart from each other, and if they met in the streets they often fought each other.

The fifth group were the police, under Social-Democratic control in Prussia and a few other *Länder,* but already strongly influenced by Nazi or nationalist officers in others. They carried out their job of enforcing law and order with great zest where the troublemakers were the Communists, and not so energetically when faced by the SA. The German police carried pistols at all times, but they had orders to use their rubber truncheons as much as possible. Once I was reporting on a mass demonstration near the Alexanderplatz; for some reason a policeman took a dislike to me, and I found myself running as fast as I could along a back street, chased by him with his truncheon drawn. Luckily he was an unusually fat little policeman, and in the end he gave up.

Who were the fighters in those civil-war armies? Brawls between SA and *Rotfront* had been going on for a few years, but with the big rise in unemployment during 1930 the ranks of all these groups swelled enormously. The life of a middle-aged jobless worker or employee was sad enough, but that of a young one was often intolerable. On dole days he had to join an endless queue outside his labour exchange, waiting for hours for his turn. In the evenings he might have lounged with his girl on a park bench, or cuddled her at a dark street corner; he had no money to take her to a café or bar. But those political organizations offered him some kind of social life at the end of the day, a uniform which made him feel important, and perhaps a plate of soup or a *Stulle,* a sandwich, by courtesy of the movement. The evening usually began with a get-together and a pep talk by some propaganda officer at the local headquarters – the backroom of a pub – and then the men went on a 'patrol' of the district, looking for trouble.

It did not matter much to these lads what the political persuasion of the movement was so long as they could use it as a vent for their natural aggression and for their anger about the miserable life on the dole, for their contempt of the authorities' bungling and impotence in the face of Germany's unholy mess. They were straining for a fight, and as a rule they got it because their opposite numbers wanted it too. And for all of them, outwitting the police was an additional bit of fun.

Most of these activities were local affairs, restricted to working-class areas. But at demonstrations and at the end of mass meetings, street battles were almost inevitable as opposing groups were bringing in their men from all over the area – one group provided guards for protecting speakers and sympathizers, another sent in its members to start counter-demonstrations or break up the meeting. I remember one such encounter which ended in bloodshed. The Communists had organized a demonstration at their party headquarters, the Karl Liebknecht House, in the eastern part of Berlin where they were numerically strong. The police appeared and behaved, so far as I could judge, somewhat aggressively; the crowd attacked them, and three officers were killed. Now there were shots, some being fired from roofs and windows. The police brought up its riot squads with searchlights, houses were raided, basements and roofs combed. Ambulances carried off about twenty injured, among them some women and children. Many arrests were made, and the next day the courts were busy trying suspected rioters.

As a rule, Communist offenders got heavy sentences while Nazis were either acquitted or let off with fines (the party paid them). Propaganda chief Goebbels could, unpunished, incite his SA in the *Angriff:* 'Hoist the flag of rebellion and resistance!' The stormtroopers obliged. *Reichsbanner* centres were attacked in Berlin and the provinces; there were many casualties. The attackers were either Nazis or *Stahlhelm* members; knives and pistols were used, and bombs began to be thrown in the countryside.

It was rioting farmers who threw them. They had founded a new Nazi organization, the 'Country People's Movement'. In some Prussian regions they carried black flags nailed to scythes and smashed up tax offices, injuring civil servants. A group of them – they were never caught – planted a bomb in the Berlin *Reichstag* building.

The armed forces were now being drawn into party politics; the Nazis made special efforts to win over *Reichswehr* officers. The Supreme Court at Leipzig had to deal with the case of three lieutenants of the garrison at Ulm, Württemberg, who had been travelling around Germany inciting young fellow-officers in other garrisons to resist the 'poisoning of the army with pacifist ideas' by the Reichs government. At the trial, Hitler was called as a witness, which offered him a wonderful opportunity for making an hour-long propaganda speech. He repeated what he had already declared on other occasions: that 'heads will fall after the victory of our movement'. The presiding judge was too startled to think of a reply to that bloodthirsty threat, and the witness was not even rebuked. The Nazis who filled the public gallery broke into enthusiastic applause. The three accused got eighteen months' confinement in a fortress, surely not a very severe sentence for conspiracy to commit high treason.

It was the only treason trial of right-wing conspirators held during the last years of the Republic. Significantly, the mild sentence was passed only a day or so after the *Reichstag* elections of September 14, 1930. Their results were a terrible shock. The NSDAP got over $6^1/_2$ million votes – 18.2 per cent, as compared with 2.8 per cent only two years earlier – and 107 seats out of 577. Hitler's party was now the second strongest after the Social Democrats; what the figures showed us was that the Nazis had gained most of their new votes from the other right-wing parties. The Social Democrats had lost only 10 seats, but the Communists had increased the number of theirs from 54 to 77. Clearly, unemployment and impoverishment had turned many German voters into radicals.

At the opening of the new *Reichstag* session, all Nazi MPs appeared in their brown uniforms; the scene looked almost like a *Sportpalast* rally.

The immediate result of the elections was yet another economic crisis. There was a crash at Berlin's stock exchange, much capital was slipping out of Germany, foreign credits were cancelled. Within a few weeks, the Reichs Bank lost a thousand million marks of its gold and currency reserves. Three months after the elections, Germany had $4^1/_2$ million unemployed; within just over a year, the six-million mark was reached.

During that year, 1931, things went from bad to worse. I cannot remember a single event which gave us any hope at all that the Republic could still be saved, except by a miracle. Chancellor Brüning was certainly no miracle man. He made old Hindenburg sign one emergency decree after the other; one of them reduced the dole for the jobless.

1931 was also the year in which we nearly got rid of Hitler, according to the surprising story I was told when I was in Munich in the autumn. My editor had called a meeting of all correspondents and contributors to discuss the journal's policy: what could we do to keep our readers from deserting the cause of the Republic, to give them more faith in democracy? We didn't get very far; the sad fact was that any direct attack on the Nazis would have cost us subscribers as well as advertisers – it had happened to other non-party newspapers.

On the last afternoon of my stay I went on a nostalgic tramride to the house where I had lived with my parents; it was in Bogenhausen, only a stone's throw from the Prince-Regent Theatre built for Wagnerian and other ambitious productions. The caretaker of our block of flats was still around. 'Have you heard?' he asked. 'That business over there, in number 16?'

I had not heard, and he told me what he knew. Prinzregentenplatz no 16 was Hitler's *pied-à-terre* in Munich; there he had rented a flat several years earlier, and invited in 1928 his teenage niece Angela Raubal, 'Geli', to live with him. Officially she was his housekeeper; in fact she was his great love. Geli was the attractive daughter of his half-sister, and one of the few members of his family he did not hate. In 1931, when he was 43, Geli was only 19 and devoted to him.

Shortly before my visit to Bogenhausen in that September there had been a tragedy. Geli – pregnant by Hitler, as it turned out – had killed herself, probably because she had found out about his friendship with Eva Braun whom he had met two years earlier. Hitler was summoned from Berlin, and Rudolf Hess went with him to the flat. There Hitler broke down. He drew his revolver to shoot himself; Hess struggled with him and took the weapon away.

It was the grief over Geli's death which gave Eva Braun her great chance. She nursed him, comforted him, put him on his feet again. Yet he cannot have shown his gratitude very much because Eva, too, made a suicide attempt only a year later by shooting herself in the neck (and again, in 1935, by taking an overdose of vanodorm). Geli remained Hitler's great dead love, despite his extensive sex life. Nazi propaganda always tried to imply that Hitler had no room for the love of women in his heart, only for love of the fatherland; some psychologists even concluded that he lived sexless – because of his habit of keeping his hands folded on his crotch as though shielding it.

But I happened to know that he had an affair, among many others, with Gretl Slezak, the sister of a classmate of mine who later became a successful film actor in Hollywood; their mother, married to the famous opera singer Leo Slezak, was Jewish, which Hitler must have known but disregarded. Another intimate friend of his, according to what I was told, was the wife of a piano manufacturer; then there were 'Putzi' Hanfstaengl's sister Erna, a Princess von Hohenlohe, Unity Mitford, a former Austrian nun who had a child by him, the daughter of a US Ambassador in Berlin, perhaps Leni Riefenstahl, and the sister of his private chauffeur, to mention but a few. He was sexually normal all right.

Germany was secretly rearming in the late 1920s. Not, of course, with the help and blessing of the government, but there were *Reichswehr* generals who had taken matters into their own hands, and hidden state funds for financing a 'black' *Reichswehr*. Occasional revelations about these activities, which were a breach of the peace treaty, were stopped by the courts, and the journalists who made them were prosecuted for treason. The Weimar Republic even started building a secret air force without anybody but a small group of officers and technicians knowing about it. The matter was disclosed for the first and only time in the *Weltbühne* ('The World's Stage'), the leading weekly of the left-wing and democratic intellectuals. The consequences were tragic.

The journal had been founded in 1905 by stage-struck young Siegfried Jacobsohn, the son of a small-time Jewish businessman. He was a brilliant, ruthlessly sincere theatre critic (once an actress whom he had slated ambushed the undersized man in a Berlin theatre foyer and gave him a hiding with her umbrella). The First World War affected Jacobsohn deeply. 'May my hand rot,' he wrote in 1918, 'if it ever fails, even for a single week, to hammer the wickedness of war and of its advocates into my fellow-men's minds — the wickedness of those advocates who are already howling for vengeance.'

From then on, the *Weltbühne* made politics its principal concern. Its circulation multiplied tenfold between 1918 and 1926, when Jacobsohn died, leaving it in the hands of some of the best, most forceful, and sincerely committed writers among the younger generation. Kurt Tucholsky was one of them, though he moved to Paris and contributed his weekly anti-Nazi, anti-militarist verses from there, while Carl von Ossietzky, the scion of an old aristocratic Prussian family, stepped into Jacobsohn's shoes as the editor. Most of Ossietzky's ancestors had been officers, except his father, a sculptor and enthusiastic Socialist whose influence on the young man's mind was decisive. In 1913, he married an English girl, Maud Woods, born at Hyderabad, the daughter of a Dragoon Guards officer.

Ossietzky was an anglophile, and so was Edith Jacobsohn, Siegfried's widow. She founded, together with her English-language teacher, a publishing firm for children's books, introduced Milne's *Winnie-the-Pooh* and Lofting's *Doctor Dolittle* to the young German readers, and published Erich Kästner's classic *Emil and the Detectives*, probably the most successful modern children's book. She must have been the first hostess to make Berlin society acquainted with that unique English institution, the cocktail party. I was once honoured with an invitation; it was a splendid experience. Edith Jacobsohn, a huge woman with a monocle, presided over an assembly of all the famous people around the *Weltbühne* – Ossietzky, a small, modest man who spoke softly and wittily; Rudolf Arnheim, the 'pope' of Germany's *cinéastes,* the film critic of the journal; Kurt Tucholsky, who was on a short visit to Berlin from his French abode; Erich Kästner, who had brought his mother along. She was a simple woman who was very much out of her depth among the Berlin intelligentsia – she had come from Dresden merely to bring her Erich a change of shirts and underpants.

Shortly after that cocktail party, Ossietzky was in trouble. Under German law, every periodical publication must have a 'responsible editor', who has to answer for any offence committed by his journal, jointly with the contributor in question. In March, 1929, the economics contributor of the *Weltbühne* analysed the budget of the Reichs Ministry of Transport, and discovered that there existed secret departments which were developing and building military aircraft – strictly forbidden under the Versailles Treaty. What he had found out was, in fact, the clandestine birth of the *Luftwaffe.*

Editor and contributor were charged with high treason and betrayal of military secrets. For two years, various courts dealt with the case; at last, late in 1931, the Supreme Court in Leipzig arrived at a verdict and sentence: both were guilty as charged, both were given prison sentences of 18 months each but remained free on bail while an appeal for remission was submitted to President Hindenburg. It was refused. The contributor got cold feet and fled to France. Friends advised Ossietzky also to go abroad, but he replied, 'A critic of matters at home who has left the country will soon be talking into empty space. If you want to fight the poisonous spirit in your homeland you must share its general destiny.'

One May morning in 1932, a sad little group gathered on the outskirts of Berlin near the high brick walls of the prison of Tegel, where Ossietzky was to serve his sentence. His friends, mostly writers and journalists, had come to say farewell to him. Ernst Toller, the poet and playwright, made a short speech, wishing him the best of luck and strength to survive the ordeal. Ossietzky answered: he was going to jail as one of the many political prisoners who shared his fate in Germany and all over the world; and if his friends were going to campaign for his release, they should do so not just for him but for all of them.

It was a hard time for Ossietzky in prison, not least because the strict non-smoking regulation made the chain-smoker miss his cigarettes. In December, 1932, however, there was an amnesty for political prisoners, and he got free just in time for Christmas.

Now he had a last chance to get out. Again the courageous man refused. As was to be expected, he was among the many anti-Nazis on Hitler's black list. In the night of the *Reichstag* fire he was taken away and sent to one of the new concentration camps.

Few pictures from the early years of Hitler Germany were more moving, more sinister, and more significant than a photograph taken at the Esterwegen concentration camp; I saw it in an illustrated Nazi weekly where it was one of a series purporting to show how the enemies of the new regime were receiving 'corrective treatment'. There was the short, slight figure of a man in his mid-forties with the high forehead of an intellectual, clad in a dark prison uniform, a number plate pinned to his chest. He was obviously trying to stand to attention, his eyes downcast, before a large bully of an SS man who had planted himself in front of him, his hands propped against his hips at an arrogant angle. One could almost hear him snarl, 'We'll finish you off yet, just you wait!'

The prisoner was Carl von Ossietzky, and they did finish him off, though it took them five more years. Already in 1934, his name was suggested to the Nobel Committee in Oslo which decided on the Peace Prize; the vigorous leader of the campaign for Ossietzky in Norway was a young Social-Democratic refugee by the name of Willy Brandt. But Ossietzky's nomination came too late, and that year the Peace Prize was awarded to the British statesman Arthur Henderson. The next chance was the Prize for 1935.

While the campaign for Ossietzky intensified all over the world – it was hoped that the award might get him out and save his life – the Swiss historian and diplomat Carl Jacob Burckhardt led a Red Cross delegation to the camp. He found Ossietzky in a dreadful condition, beaten up, very sick, 'no longer able to feel anything'. Burckhardt asked him whether he had any messages for his friends. 'Thanks,' he whispered. 'Tell them I am at the end. It will soon be over. It's all right that way.' And he added, 'I only wanted peace.'

The Nobel Committee was not to be hurried. No Peace Prize for 1935 was awarded at all. In 1936, one thousand prominent men of the western world – among them Albert Einstein, Thomas Mann, Wickham Steed – urged the Committee to make haste and award him the prize. One single voice spoke against him: that of the Norwegian writer Knut Hamsun, now in his dotage and a victim of Nazi propaganda.

In November, 1936, Ossietzky got the Peace Prize. The Nazis had to let him go. He was in an advanced stage of tuberculosis. His wife Maud received the money; some con-man tricked her out of it. Still, Ossietzky was able to get treatment in Switzerland. He lingered on for another year and a half. In the spring of 1938 he died in Berlin. Very few of his friends were still around to attend the cremation. A Gestapo man was there, too, and took their names.

Hitler seemed to have recovered quickly from his depression about Geli's suicide, for a few weeks later he was working hard on a new political plot. Hugenberg had organized a great demonstration of the major right-wing forces at the popular spa Bad Harzburg, and Hitler agreed to unite with the German National Party and the *Stahlhelm* in a common front against the Brüning government. There was an impressive parade of stormtroopers; some Hohenzollern princes and many former officers were amongst the invited guests. A surprise speaker was Dr Hjalmar Schacht, the 'financial wizard' of the inflation and former Democrat, who now called himself a 'worried patriot'; he railed at the whole Weimar system with its 'hypocrisy, lawlessness, and impotence'. He was obviously expecting to secure for himself an important ministerial post in a future Hugenberg–Hitler government.

Hitler's aim with that 'Harzburg Front', as the alliance came to be called, was to get Hugenberg to guarantee him the post of Reichs Chancellor after Brüning's overthrow, while Hugenberg was still hoping to climb to power himself with the help of the Nazi movement. Each of the two men was confident of making the other his stooge. The result of Harzburg was a formal alliance of partners with mutually exclusive aims.

Yet Brüning held on until the early spring of 1932. With his emergency decrees he tried to reduce the cost of living, and he created a new government post, that of 'Reichs Commissar for Price Control'. The man he picked for it was Carl Friedrich Goerdeler, Mayor of Leipzig – the same Goerdeler who was going to be hanged by the Nazis as a participant of the unsuccessful officers' putsch against Hitler in July, 1944.

Seven years had gone by since Hindenburg's election as President, and a new vote was due. Brüning and his *Zentrum* party backed Hindenburg's re-election; the Communists put up their party leader, Ernst Thälmann; the nationalists nominated a nonentity from the *Stahlhelm* as their candidate, and the Nazis put up Hitler: the 'Harzburg Front' had been unable to agree on a common candidate. At the election in March, 1932, the necessary majority was not reached by any of the candidates, and a second poll was required a month later. The Social Democrats decided to back Hindenburg; their slogan was as absurd as it was unwise: Vote for Hindenburg as the 'lesser evil', compared to Hitler. It shocked millions of loyal Social Democrats who never forgave their party for what they regarded as a betrayal of its principles. Predictably, Hindenburg was re-elected with nearly 20 million votes.

Another six weeks later, right-wing pressure on Hindenburg had grown so strong that he had to dismiss Brüning and appoint as the new Chancellor a representative of Germany's most reactionary class – the aristocratic Prussian *Junkers*. That man, Franz von Papen, turned out to be the most effective of all the gravediggers of the Republic.

Born in Westphalia as the scion of a wealthy, Catholic, land-owning family, he had joined the army and attained the rank of major in the cavalry. But he was spared service in the first World War as he was instead appointed military attaché at the German Embassy in Washington. His spell of duty in this capacity, however, was cut short even before America's entry into the war when he negligently left his attaché case in the New York subway – complete with documents about German plots to blow up American munitions factories and carry out sabotage acts and bomb attacks. There had always been a strong suspicion that Papen's agents had thrown a bomb during the San Francisco 'Preparedness Parade' in 1916, a crime for which a well-known trade union leader, Tom Mooney, had to spend 22 years in San Quentin prison, convicted on flimsy evidence.

Papen spent the rest of the war as chief of the general staff of the Turkish army in Palestine; there it was General Allenby who cut his career short. Back in Germany, he entered the Prussian parliament as a *Zentrum* member in 1921. But his claim to fame was the foundation of the *Herrenklub*, the 'gentlemen's club', in Berlin. We used to show our visiting friends its magnificent premises near the Brandenburg Gate. It was much more than a social club: it was an exclusive circle of aristocrats with rightist political ambitions. The newspapers used to call them the '*Almanac de Gotha* shadow cabinet'.

Papen was a 'gentleman rider' in sports, an old-fashioned nob in the *salon*, and an unscrupulous intriguer in politics. The French Ambassador in Berlin, François-Poncet, a shrewd observer of the 1932 scene, reported that Papen was being called a bungler and deceiver, shallow, vain, and cunning. But he was on first-name terms with another Prussian officer and aristocrat, bald-headed General Kurt von Schleicher, whom Hindenburg trusted; and it had been 'Kurtchen' who recommended 'Fränzchen' to the President as the new Chancellor. Other cabinet appointments went to other aristocratic reactionaries, most of them without any experience in government affairs; the notable exception was Herr von Neurath, who was recalled from his post as German ambassador in London to become Foreign Minister. The *Herrenklub* was in power.

But Germany's largest *Land*, Prussia, still had a Social-Democratic government, backed by its parliament, the *Landtag*. These Prussian ministers were as many thorns in the flesh of the new nationalist Reichs ministers; they had to be removed. Papen did it in true aristocratic fashion. He made Hindenburg sign a decree appointing him, Papen, 'Reichs Commissar for Prussia', replacing the elected Prussian government. It was a flagrant breach of the Weimar Constitution. On July 20, 1932, Schleicher, now *Reichswehr* Minister, ordered his Berlin garrison commander, General von Rundstedt, to take the 'necessary action'. This consisted in sending, early one morning, an officer and a few *Reichswehr* soldiers to the Prussian Ministry of the Interior in the boulevard Unter den Linden. They found the Minister, Carl Severing, in his office, and ordered him to leave, threatening to use force. Severing did not resist, but declared that he was going 'under duress to avoid bloodshed', and went. Just as meekly and unheroically behaved the rest of the Prussian ministers, who were mostly arrested in their homes and kept overnight in an officers' penitentiary.

At the *Herrenklub*, the jubilant gentlemen boasted that 'one lieutenant and three men' — a proverbial phrase — had finished off the whole 'Social-Democratic spook'. The Social-Democratic Party and the trade unions admonished their members to remain calm in the face of this outrage of the Papen clique. The Communists' call for a general strike was ignored.

Those of us who had still believed in the staying power of Germany's largest party — this was what the Social Democrats still were — felt betrayed and forsaken. They had been the creators and guardians of our Constitution, and now they had given in to unconstitutional force, yielding their offices without a fight and with hardly a murmur. The end of the Republic seemed near.

At least for one day we still had a good laugh even in those depressing weeks. Papen had appointed a friend of his, the Mayor of Essen, Dr Bracht, as his Vice-Commissar for Prussia; Bracht had taken a leading executive part in the removal of the Prussian government. But his legislative genius shone only once — when he issued, in the midst of summer, a new regulation concerning men's and women's bathing costumes: they were now required to have a triangular gusset in that sensitive place where the onlookers might have discerned the difference of the sexes.

I remember 1932 most of all as the year of continual elections. First the two presidential ones; then Papen made Hindenburg dissolve the *Reichstag*, and a new one was elected in July. This election brought another victory for the Nazis. Nearly 14 million voted for them, which made them the strongest party in the *Reichstag*, with 230 seats. The Social Democrats had lost heavily; they polled only eight million votes and got 133 seats. Clearly, their spineless behaviour in Prussia had undermined the confidence of millions of their former followers. The Communists gained; their five million votes brought them 89 seats.

Still, it is worth noting that the NSDAP got only 37.3 per cent of the total vote – the most it ever obtained in a free election.

I was in the press gallery at the opening session. As the largest party, the NSDAP had the right to nominate the *Reichstag* President – equivalent to the Speaker in the British House of Commons – from their MPs. They chose Hermann Goering. He was formally elected and mounted the raised seat of his new office, with the innumerable medals on his chest tinkling. But before Goering's installation there was an odd interlude: a Communist made the first speech of the session, 75-year-old Klara Zetkin, the *Alterspräsidentin* or 'Mother' of the House, who had the traditional right to open proceedings. With a shaky, dying voice she affirmed her faith in a future Soviet Germany. It was a pathetic scene. The Nazi members, again in their brown or black uniforms, kept quiet; no doubt they had been ordered by their leaders to avoid any incidents that might end in brawls and result in another dissolution of the *Reichstag* and a new general election. Yet this happened all the same within a few months.

For a short period, Brüning had forbidden the wearing of party uniforms in public; even the two civil-war organizations of the Nazis, the SA and SS, had been banned for a while. When Brüning went, these restrictions – which he had never been able to enforce effectively – went with him. There was a flare-up of guerilla warfare in all parts of Germany, with increased

162

brutality. Now the stormtroopers were using firearms everywhere; their targets were not just *Reichsbanner* and *Rotfront* men in the streets and their assembly centres but buildings such as the Berlin publishing offices of the *Vorwärts*, the Social-Democratic party organ; in Munich they tried to invade the house of the Bavarian Prime Minister; trade-union headquarters were stormed and ransacked all over the country. The worst incident happened in a small town in Silesia, where 27 people were killed and 180 badly injured by shots. In Altona, Hamburg's working-class district, 14 were killed in a gunfight between Nazis and Communists. In the night after the July elections, the East Prussian capital, Königsberg, was the scene of several murders by the SA; a former police chief and a town councillor were shot in their beds. In Upper Silesia, stormtroopers broke into the home of a Communist worker and trampled him to death in front of his mother; the five culprits were sentenced to death by a courageous judge at Beuthen — a most unusual sentence in 1932, and it had an unusual sequel: Hitler practically declared war on Chancellor Papen, whom he blamed for the Beuthen judgment. 'Now I know your so-called objectivity', he said in an open telegram. 'The seed that is now growing will no longer be stunted by penalties.'

Incredible as it may seem, considering the murderous fight between the Nazis and the Communists, there was a certain amount of tactical co-operation of the two parties; after all, they were both trying to topple the Weimar system, and their common enemies were the Social Democrats. In the *Reichstag*, the Nazis and the Communists together had now the absolute majority, and they joined forces to oppose any motions tabled by the Social Democrats, or to push through acts which benefited them both, such as an amnesty for political prisoners. This was the amnesty that freed Ossietzky at Christmas, 1932.

One evening in October, a Communist neighbour of mine, a young unemployed worker called Hans (I never knew his surname) asked me to come with him to witness an 'interesting demonstration' in our suburban district. He took me to the tramway depot. There, Hans' comrades and SA men were busy preventing the tramcars from leaving — both their parties had called an unofficial strike against the Social-Democratic management of the Berlin public-transport corporation which had reduced wages by 2 *pfennig* an hour. The Communists were cutting the ropes of the overhead pickup arms of the cars while the Nazis were pouring cement into the rails.

At that time, some left-wing intellectuals who lived in our residential area became worried about their safety as SA attacks on homes grew more frequent. We tried to recruit sympathizers for a kind of vigilantes group for mutual help in emergencies; the co-operation of our prominent neighbours seemed to us important, and we asked the famous *Weltbühne* film critic, Rudolf Arnheim, to join us. Militant though he was in his writings, he wanted to be left alone in daily life. Our disappointment in him was even greater when we heard, a few months later, that he had emigrated to Mussolini's Fascist Italy.

Hans brought me a pistol for self-protection. I never used it and got rid of it later when its possession might have meant arrest and concentration camp. I was no hero. Hans, too, was a disappointment. One day I passed a troop of marching storm troopers in the street, and there was Hans in a brand new brown uniform. He looked the other way when he saw me. It was a small but characteristic symptom of the way things were going in those last months of 1932. A much larger one, which many of us felt as a personal blow, was Max Reinhardt's sudden decision to abandon his five theatres in Berlin and move – it was not yet called 'emigrate' – to Vienna.

In November came the last election of 1932. Papen the gentleman rider had come a cropper. He had fallen out with Hitler after that aggressive telegram. The *Länder* governments, particularly Bavaria, had the gravest misgivings about Papen's intentions since his coup against the Prussian government. In the end, even his own *Zentrum* party and its affiliated Christian trade unions gave him to understand that they would no longer put up with his high-handed, authoritarian manner. His scanty *Reichstag* backing, consisting of the *Zentrum* and the right-wing parties, was falling to pieces; but there was not yet any other way of forming a government except by coalition – the price which every country with proportional representation voting has to pay for this, no doubt equitable, system of parliamentary election.

Reluctantly, Hindenburg accepted Papen's resignation, and the *Reichstag* was again dissolved.

The November elections brought one sensational result. For the first time since their participation in the parliamentary game, the Nazis lost votes – in fact, no less than two million, 6.2 per cent of all votes. This cost them 34 seats, yet they remained the strongest party in the Reichstag, for the Social Democrats had lost even more, about 10 per cent. There were all kinds of interpretations of these results. The most obvious one seemed to be that the Hitler movement had past its peak, possibly because of the murderous civil war the SA gangs were carrying on; at any rate, the widespread, almost hypnotic belief in the *Führer*'s invincibility, his irresistible rise was shattered. There was now at last some hope that Hitler was not inevitable.

But what about the calamity of the Social Democrats? My Munich editor wanted to know what the Social-Democratic Party in the *Reichstag* were feeling about it all, and I tried to get an interview with the prominent MP, Rudolf Breitscheid. He was unavailable, but he sent me his son, also an MP.

We met in the lobby of the heavily ornate *Reichstag* building, still topped by the old imperial crown above its dome. Young Breitscheid – he was in his early 30s – reclined on one of the ancient, tatty leather settees, and put his feet up. He radiated lofty confidence. The Nazis? Obviously finished. But what about his own party?

'What about it?' he replied. 'All right, we lost ten per cent this time. We'll gain ten per cent the next time, you can be sure.'

I wasn't, especially not after that interview. It was the most discouraging one of my career.

Soon afterwards came my most superfluous interview. Tom Mooney, the imprisoned American trade-unionist, had appealed against his sentence, offering new evidence that he did not throw that bomb in 1916. There was one man who could have spoken up for him: Herr von Papen. My editor wanted me to see him and ask him to help Mooney by admitting, after all that time, that German agents had been responsible. I did not expect much from that interview, but I went dutifully to Papen, now out of office but still working in the Wilhelmstrasse.

He was a gaunt, haughty man with a rigid face, a most unpleasant type. I tried to make him say something about his time as a military attaché in Washington. He replied merely Yes or No to my questions. Then I mentioned, cautiously, the name of

Tom Mooney. 'Never heard of him,' he said and got up. End of interview.

Something was going on behind the scenes of the Wilhelmstrasse, the *Herrenklub*, the Nazi headquarters. Even my well-informed journalistic colleagues could merely guess what. We knew the characters of the drama but we had to form our own conclusions about what they were up to; rumours abounded in those days — and some which we discarded as absurd later turned out to have been tragically true. It is only in the light of more recent revelations that one can put the jigsaw puzzle of December 1932 and January 1933 together, though a few pieces may still be missing, never to be found.

Hitler had a troubled time. He was worried not only about his losses in the election but much more about his row with Gregor Strasser, the leading Socialist among the National-Socialist ideologists. He had been Hitler's close friend since 1924 and done an excellent administrative job in organizing the NSDAP. Hitler's hob-nobbing with aristocrats and industrialists had angered him for a long time; 'German Socialism', Strasser's pet concept, had disappeared from the party's propaganda because Hitler did not want to alarm his new friends, especially as he was again in desperate need of money. Things came to a head between him and Strasser, and Strasser left the party, resigning from all his offices. Hitler, it was said, talked again about killing himself. At a public meeting he broke into tears when he spoke about Strasser's 'treason'. It was Papen who saved him; or rather Papen's own attempt to climb back into the saddle.

Papen tried to persuade Hindenburg to give him another chance as Chancellor. His idea was to disregard the parties, shunt the whole *Reichstag* on a dead-end track and rule autocratically without any regard for the Constitution. The attempt failed because even the members of his own former cabinet refused to go along with him. Hindenburg now decided in favour of his fellow-officer Schleicher as Papen's successor.

Schleicher accepted. Early in December, he formed his cabinet mainly from the ranks of Papen's gentlemen, including Neurath as Foreign Minister and Dr Bracht, of gusset fame, as Minister of the Interior. Schleicher also tried to get Strasser, the renegade Nazi, to work out a programme for providing jobs —

The two main gravediggers of the Weimar Republic: Franz von Papen and General von Schleicher at the races in the autumn of 1932

unemployment had by now exceeded the six-million mark. But the trade unions refused to co-operate with a general and an ex-Nazi, and the whole project came to nothing.

Papen, the old fox, was determined to put a stop to the political career of his 'friend' Schleicher, now his successful rival. Both were experienced intriguers, but Papen was indubitably the more cunning and reckless of the two. He resorted to a trick to get back to power; the thought that he might be doing irreparable harm to his country does not seem to have entered his mind. The best way to overthrow Schleicher, he reckoned, was to use Hitler against him; and Hitler, in his present difficulties, could be bought at a bargain price.

On January 5, 1933, the morning papers reported an amazing story. The previous day, Papen had brought Hitler, accompanied by Hess and Himmler, to the house of the immensely rich industrial banker, von Schröder, in Cologne. As Schröder himself said later, Papen put before him a plan to form a new government led by Hitler and himself — as though the banker were the Reichs President. Hitler declared, as he had done several times in the past, that he would take part in a cabinet only if he were given the post of Chancellor; Papen's idea of a two-man team of leaders was unacceptable. Papen and his ministerial nominees would have to co-operate in Hitler's terms. All right, said Papen, but he himself would insist on being Vice-Chancellor — he was obviously still hoping to bring Hitler under control. Schröder and the other representatives of powerful economic interests, whom he had invited to the meeting, agreed and promised their support.

The meeting was, of course, meant to be kept secret; but it was not only leaked to the press, even photographers had been tipped off, and pictures of Papen entering Schröder's house were in the papers. I heard that Schleicher, who had his spies everywhere, had done the leaking and tipping. Yet he did nothing to counteract Papen's and Hitler's plans; perhaps he did not take Papen seriously enough. Besides, Schleicher's own political troubles were mounting; he made enemies on all sides — worst of all, he fell out with the *Junkers*, Hindenburg's mighty landowning friends. On January 28, 1933, Chancellor Schleicher was forced to resign after a mere eight weeks' spell in power.

The General Field Marshal and the ex-Corporal: Hindenburg
shakes Hitler's hand after appointing him Reichs Chancellor.
Behind them (centre) Admiral Raeder, (left) Goering, (far left)
Goebbels

169

Like a shot, Papen rushed to Hindenburg. At first, the President and his advisers were reluctant to agree to a Papen-Hitler government; there was still the General Field-Marshal's dislike of the 'Bohemian corporal' to overcome. Then, suddenly, another 'leak' – possibly inspired by Papen – made him give in : Schleicher, it was rumoured, was planning a coup with the help of the Potsdam garrison; Hindenburg's son and perhaps Hindenburg himself were to be arrested, and Schleicher would make himself dictator of Germany. It was an unlikely story, but the President dropped his intention of re-appointing Schleicher. Papen assured Hindenburg that the majority of his cabinet would be reliable nationalists, including Hugenberg, and there would be no more than three National Socialists. He had indeed got Hitler 'cheap' – or so he thought.

And so, on Monday, January 30, at 11 o'clock in the morning, Hindenburg received Hitler, Papen, and the whole of their cabinet: Hitler as Chancellor, Papen as Vice-Chancellor, Neurath as Foreign Minister, Hugenberg as Minister for Economy and Agriculture, Goering for Air Transport, and Hitler's trusted crony Wilhelm Frick for the important Ministry of the Interior, which of course included the police. They were all sworn in at once by the President on the Constitution – the Weimar Constitution in which none of them believed.

For the benefit of the photographers and the German public at large, Hindenburg and Hitler drove to Potsdam to enact their 'historical' handshake against the backdrop of Prussia's glorious past.

Epilogue
WEIMAR'S FUNERAL PYRE

In the afternoon of that 30 of January, 1933, I set out on a tour of Berlin in my car. It was my journalistic duty to record the town's reaction, and especially that of the parties, to the momentous news we had heard on the radio, and which we could read as a two-word headline of the special editions of the newspapers now being sold in the streets: *HITLER REICHSKANZLER*. I also had the hope that somehow my tour would allay my feeling of catastrophe and cataclysm; perhaps it was just a personal over-reaction after all these weeks and months of anxiety – perhaps it did not, after all, mean the end of the world, our world, that Adolf Hitler was heading a new government.

The streets were uncannily quiet, as though the Berliners had been stunned by the news; or they were worn out by that winter of unemployment and misery: any change, they might have felt, would be better than no change at all. Brüning, Papen, Schleicher – none of them had, as Chancellors, done anything to help the people.

I don't remember exactly what I found at the headquarters of the *Zentrum* and the small middle-of-the-road Democratic Party; the bell had obviously tolled for them, but they did not realize or admit it. All I recall is: silence at their party offices. I drove on to the Communist headquarters, the Karl Liebknecht House. Here, the gates were firmly locked, with guards of *Rotfront* men behind them, ready to fight off any attacks. Outside, in the square, groups of Communists were discussing hastily printed leaflets with the outsize headline: 'General Strike!'

It seemed, on that day, the only way of stopping and toppling the Hitler government before it could establish itself firmly and get a grip on the *Länder* governments, the *Reichswehr*, the provincial police forces. Without trains, without communications, without supplies it would have been unable to govern. But a general strike would have been possible only with the co-operation of the Social Democrats and their trade unions. I drove on to the *Vorwärts* building: there the printing presses were bound to have produced leaflets with some kind of indication of the party's and the unions' attitude.

They had indeed. Outside the gates, which were also locked and guarded, *Reichsbanner* men were distributing leaflets. They read 'Keep calm! Don't let them provoke you!' I found a party official and asked him to explain that slogan. Nothing hasty should be done, that was the party policy, he told me. Let the Nazi and nationalist government stew in their own juice, let them flounder and fail. What about a general strike as the Communists wanted it, I asked. Never, he said; we cannot join them, all they want is a Communist dictatorship. He wouldn't be seen dead in their company. But why can't your own unions call a general strike, I asked. He hesitated. 'Some of our functionaries have suggested it,' he admitted. 'But a general strike at this point in time would mean wasting the munition of the working class. Let's wait and see.' This was exactly what the *Vorwärts* wrote in its next issue. It also published the grand new slogan for Germany's working class, devised by the party boss, Breitscheid senior: 'Be prepared!' What for, he unfortunately forgot to say.

I turned back, even more depressed than when I had set out. Surely the Social-Democratic Party and the trade unions were missing their final chance of survival – or at least of making a last courageous stand. Millions of Germans must have been waiting at this moment for some rallying call, some signal for attack or resistance. It did not come; and it has never been in the nature of the German people to march or fight without leadership, to act without an order or call from above. The new men in the Wilhelmstrasse knew this instinctively: they were grouped around a leader who would tell the people what to do, and the Germans' conditioned reflex was to obey.

On my drive home, through the darkening, wintry streets, I passed large groups of uniformed stormtroopers on foot and in lorries, making their way to the government district. An hour or so later, radio reporters described the scene in the Wilhelmstrasse. The whole of Berlin's SA had been mobilized for a victory parade with flags and torchlights. Hitler, his ministers, and the inner circle of his party stood at the windows of the Chancellery, bathing in the glory of thousands of torch flames. At the window of his own *palais,* the Reichs President watched the procession, listening to the old military marches played by the bands. We never knew what he thought of it all. But the next day, Berliners told each other that old Hindenburg had been shaking his head, lost in wonder, while his mind was slipping back to the battlefields of the past; and he said, 'Amazing – so many Russian prisoners!'

That was the last joke I ever heard about Reichs President Hindenburg.

There were as yet no large-scale arrests during the first few days of the new regime, but a good many people took no chances and packed their bags at once. Among those who left Germany in a hurry were politicians who had been consistently attacked in the Nazi papers; left-wing writers and artists; prominent Communists who feared that the party policy of staying and 'going underground' would not save them from being hunted down and arrested. The frontiers were still open; the border guards had probably not yet been instructed to stop certain travellers from leaving the country. What we did not know was that 'Wanted' lists were already being drawn up, and that at Oranienburg, a little town north of Berlin, and at Dachau, north of Munich, the first concentration camps were being built.

The arrests made by the new regime were at first a rather haphazard affair, especially in the provinces, where local Nazi bosses sent their stormtroopers and/or police around the towns to pick up all with whom they had axes to grind. In Munich, practically the whole staff of the publishing house for which I worked as Berlin correspondent was taken into 'protective custody', as arbitrary arrests were now called, and locked up in the main Munich prison of Stadelheim. There they remained for nine months while the entire firm was staffed with Nazi party members. Among those thus robbed of their livelihood were the firm's chairman who had been involved in the stab-in-the-back controversy, and a young Hungarian editor who, after his release, emigrated to London where he started *Lilliput* and *Pic-*

173

ture Post. One staff member of the publishing house, a completely non-political music critic, was murdered by the SA; it turned out that they had mistaken him for someone else with the same surname.

My work for the Munich journal had of course come to an end. I had no idea whether I was on any 'black list', though the SS organ had attacked me once or twice because of articles of mine they didn't like. It was no easy decision: should one take the risk and stay in Germany, or go abroad, into an uncertain future, soon to be dependent on charity? Then there also was the feeling that we anti-Nazis should not make things easier for Hitler by emigrating – that we could do more against him inside the country than outside it.

I decided to stay and joined one of the many 'underground' groups which were now springing up. We met once or twice a week in the surgery of a dentist to discuss events, exchange information, work out leaflets. I still shudder when I think of our complete lack of experience, our utter carelessness with which we went about our anti-Nazi activities; none of us, for instance, thought of the possibility that our group might have been infiltrated by a Nazi spy. By sheer good luck we were not caught.

Professionally, too, I was lucky. The Berlin office of the *New York Times* feature service, which employed a number of journalists and photographers, invited me to work for them. There was a fair chance that the new regime, still anxious to present itself as respectable to the *Ausland*, the outside world, would leave us alone. I stuck a little US flag on my car and was never molested. The German press, however, was not handled with kidgloves. On his first day in office, Dr Frick, the new Minister of the Interior, called a press conference and told the journalists that the regime considered the freedom of the press a matter of 'the greatest importance'. Three days later, the *Vorwärts* in Berlin and most of the Social-Democratic papers in the provinces were banned for a week under the pretext that they had printed an 'inflammatory' declaration by their party. The same happened to much of the *Zentrum* and the entire Communist press. The Karl Liebknecht House was raided, all meetings and demonstrations by the Communists prohibited. Yet the trade unions still ignored the Communists' frantic calls for a general strike.

Nor did the nine non-Nazi cabinet ministers lift a finger to stop their three Nazi colleagues – Hitler, Goering, and Frick – from knocking down one pillar of the democratic system after another. The nationalists, led by Papen and Hugenberg, were probably still confident that Hitler could be 'contained', that he could be kept in check in things that really mattered to them; freedom of the press did not. Hugenberg's provincial papers, all right-wing, gave no cause for concern to the new regime; they all wrote enthusiastically about it.

We could see in our private and professional lives how things were going. Suddenly, many of our acquaintances were wearing the swastika badges of the Nazi party openly on their lapels – heaven knowns how long they had been hiding them pinned to the inside. These people were now parading their allegiance to Hitler, confident that party membership would help them in business; civil servants were banking on better chance of promotion. There were, I heard, some dramatic scenes in the wings of theatres when actors turned up with swastika badges for rehearsals.

I was very much taken aback to see some half-Jews, I suppose baptized ones, sporting the badge. One of them was a man I knew very well, a literary agent who had made much money by selling my articles and those by other anti-Nazis to the provincial press. I asked him whether he was not worried that the new regime might close down his agency. 'Not at all,' he replied. 'They won't touch me. I've done them too many favours.' A few weeks later he was gone; he had emigrated to Denmark.

It seemed a matter of course that the new government dissolved the *Reichstag*, fixing general elections for March 5, 1933. It still sounded democratic, but any hope of a proper election campaign was quickly crushed. A 'Decree for the Protection of the German People', drawn up by Hitler, Frick and Papen and signed by President Hindenburg, was the government's opening shot. It curtailed freedom of assembly and of the press, thereby 'legalizing' the ban on anti-Nazi papers; strikes in public services were forbidden. Goering, who had meanwhile been given a new post, that of 'Commissioner for the Prussian Ministry of the Interior,' issued to the Prussian police a regulation which was, in effect, a licence to kill any active anti-Nazis: 'Police officers

175

who make use of their firearms in the execution of their duties will benefit by my protection.' He also replaced the police chiefs of thirteen major towns by Nazi functionaries. 'Goering is cleaning out the Augean stables,' explained Goebbels, now appointed 'Minister of Propaganda and Public Enlightenment'. Fifty thousand members of the SA, SS, and the *Stahlhelm* were enlisted as 'auxiliary police officers'.

Bavaria was the only German *Land* whose government resistęd these takeover acts by the *Reichs* regime. The men in Munich declared that they would not hand over their offices to people appointed by Berlin. There was some talk that Berlin would send some 'Commissar' to Munich to 'put things in order'. Munich declared that as soon as that Commissar crossed the border into Bavaria he would be arrested. So far as I can remember he never came; the Nazis of Munich themselves took over step by step. Still, Bavaria was the last *Land* to be 'co-ordinated' with Berlin – the new term for nazification.

To even the most non-political mind it was now clear that the Nazis' great aim was that of winning the forthcoming elections with such an overwhelming majority that the next *Reichstag* would back a government made up mainly of their party members, with no or just a few nationalists in the cabinet. It should all appear to be the German people's 'democratic' choice. By hook or by crook, the voting should be as near as possible to 100 per cent in the Nazis' favour.

Did the other parties understand what was going on? I don't think so. Hugenberg, Papen and the nationalist groups formed their own right-wing front and conducted their own election campaign, hoping to retain their numerical superiority in a future cabinet. The Social Democrats again rejected the Communists' appeal to form a united front with them; their confidence of winning back their former majority in parliament was almost pathetic. 'Berlin is not Rome,' wrote the *Vorwärts* on one of the infrequent days when the paper was not banned. 'Hitler is not Mussolini. Berlin will never be the capital of a Fascist *Reich*. Berlin remains red.'

At half-past nine on the night of Monday, February 27, 1933, I was rung at home by a *New York Times* reporter from his office in the Kochstrasse, Berlin's Fleet Street. 'There's a fire in the

Reichstag,' he said. 'We've sent our photographers there. Are you coming?'

I went by underground, expecting that the approach roads to the building would be closed to cars. And so they were, but I got through the police cordon with my press card. It was impossible, however, to get any closer; the Tiergarten, the public park, was jammed with police cars and fire-brigade vehicles. So I made my way to the north of the *Reichstag*, across the bridge over the river Spree, and from there I had an unobstructed view of the scene.

It was not just 'a fire' — the whole large building was ablaze, and the flames were belching out of the dome. The spectacle was almost awe-inspiring. For an hour or so I watched the work of the firemen, who were slowly getting the flames under control; but much of the building seemed to be gutted. I went back to the Kochstrasse to hear the latest news. How had the fire started? There was a news bulletin on the radio, just issued by the official Prussian press service. One man had been arrested in the building shortly after nine o'clock by a police constable; firelighters and petrol-soaked rags were found on him. He was identified as a 24-year-old Dutchman, a bricklayer by the name of Marinus van der Lubbe. He had, said the radio, admitted that he was a Communist and that he had been in touch with the Social Democrats. There was no doubt that van der Lubbe was one of the arsonists; his fellow conspirators were now being sought and arrested. Incriminating evidence about a Communist-Socialist plot to start a bloody rebellion and civil war, we were told, had been found at the Karl Liebknecht House already three days earlier, and the burning of the *Reichstag* was to be the signal for revolt.

Our little group of listeners in the Kochstrasse sat there, dumbfounded. That story about a revolt from the Left sounded too improbable, after all those abortive efforts to organize some form of co-operation between Communists and Social Democrats. What else was it then? Could it be a signal, given by the Nazis themselves, for the wholesale arrest, and perhaps worse, of Hitler's enemies? This fire had come too pat, just five days before the elections. It looked very much like the ghastly climax of the election campaign. None of us in the office believed for a moment that the fire was a mere coincidence.

177

Sefton Delmer, the Berlin correspondent of the London *Daily Express,* had made a point of being on good terms with the Nazi leaders. I went to his office in the small hours of the morning to hear whether he knew more. He, too, had been at the Reichstag, and on the way he had run into Alfred Rosenberg, the Nazi ideologist and now editor of the *Völkischer Beobachter*, the national daily of the party. Rosenberg, said Delmer, was rather worried and said to him, 'I only hope that this isn't the work of our chaps. It's just the sort of thing some of them might do.'

Delmer was then allowed to join a group of Nazi leaders who were watching the fire from a nearby building. Surprisingly, they all happened to be in Berlin although they had been touring the provinces, speaking at election meetings, for the past week or so. Goering was excited. 'The Communists are the culprits!' he kept shouting. He had been the first Nazi high-up on the scene. 'He would have liked to throw me out,' said Delmer, 'but then he heard Hitler say, *"Guten Abend, Herr Delmer,"* and that was my ticket of admission.' Goering reported to Hitler that he had ordered full mobilization of the regular and auxiliary police: 'We are ready for anything.'

When Papen arrived, Hitler shook his hand. 'This is a heaven-sent signal, Herr von Papen. If this fire, as I believe, is the work of the Communists, then we must destroy that murderous pest with an iron fist,' Delmer heard Hitler say. Goebbels chimed in: 'Now we have to act!' Papen soon left the Nazi group to report to President Hindenburg. 'Papen must have realized that the *Reichstag* fire put paid to any attempts at restraining Hitler, at taming and controlling the Nazis,' said Delmer.

The fire was investigated by the Political Police, soon to be renamed 'Gestapo', short for *Geheime Staatspolizei*. Rudolf Diels, head of the Political Police, told later how, in that night, Hitler gave him the cue for action. From a balcony the *Führer* had been staring at the flames. Then he suddenly turned to Diels and screamed, 'Now we'll show them! Anyone who stands in our way will be cut down! The German people have been soft for too long! Tonight, all Communist members of the *Reichstag* must be hanged, all Communist sympathizers must be locked up – and that goes for the Social Democrats, too!'

Police surveying the burnt-out Reichstag

The mass hanging was not yet practicable: what would the *Ausland* have said? But what we heard on the radio on the Tuesday was bad enough. A new 'Emergency Decree for the Protection of the People and the State' abolished the rest of the liberties of the Weimar Constitution that were still in force, at least theoretically: freedom from arbitrary arrest, freedom of speech and assembly, inviolability of letters and telephone conversations. Search warrants were no longer required, confiscation of property without legal authorization was permitted. It was the Great Charter of police dictatorship; the citizen was robbed of all protection against the power of the state. At the same time, the death penalty was introduced for any action considered to 'endanger the state', and for the disclosure of official and military secrets. The Reichs police authorities were set above those of the *Länder*.

That decree was Hitler's great breakthrough to terrorist dictatorship.

On the morning after the fire, thousands of suitcases were

hastily packed. A second wave of emigration, much larger than the first one after January 30, rolled over the borders — to Switzerland, Austria, France, Holland, Denmark. More Communist and Social-Democratic politicians, including ministers and senior officials, left-wing writers and artists, ordinary Jewish citizens and anti-Nazi Catholics were fleeing from their homeland, anxious to get out while the frontiers were still open. Many left their material possessions, their businesses behind. I tried to ring friends whom I believed to be in danger of arrest. Some of those who answered were not sure whether to stay or go; we spoke in guarded terms — the German telephone language for years to come. Often the problem was whether to leave at once alone, or prepare for the emigration of the whole family. Some of my friends made their decisions too late, and were arrested; for instance, there were several blocks of flats called the 'artists' colony' in the south-west of Berlin, which were raided by the SA one night. All the men were taken away.

The aftermath of the fire was a large-scale attempt at securing a majority for Hitler in the coming *Reichstag* by brute force and intimidation. Election candidates of anti-Nazi parties were arrested or scared into leaving the country; known leftists had to reckon with an early-morning raid by stormtroopers, and many went into hiding or at least kept their heads down and their mouths shut; ordinary voters were exposed to a barrage of Nazi propaganda during those last few days before the election, while the opposing parties had little or no chance at all to reply — for instance, to a leaflet like this:

THE REICHSTAG IN FLAMES!

Set alight by the Communists!
This is what the whole country would
look like if Communism and its ally,
Social Democracy, would come to power
only for a few months!
Innocent citizens shot as hostages!
Farmers' houses burnt down!
All Germany must join in the outcry:
Stamp out Communism!
Smash Social Democracy!
Vote for Hitler!

180

But even more effective were the stories we were now hearing and reading about Oranienburg, Dachau, and the other concentration camps which were filling up with 'enemies of the people'. The terror had begun, and it was Hitler's most savage weapon in the election fight.

Yet in spite of it all and in spite of a very high poll – nearly forty million people voted – the NSDAP did not get the absolute majority at the election but only 43.9 per cent, which gave them 162 of 422 seats. Even more surprising was the fact, evident from these figures, that the results had not been rigged. Perhaps the Nazis had been so confident in their election victory that they did not bother to intimidate the returning officers into falsifying the figures. Miraculously, the Social Democrats lost but one seat, and Hitler still needed the nationalist parties as parliamentary allies – for the time being.

It took him a few more months of brute force, of lies and decrees to eliminate all opposition to his party, and the final blow against his enemies inside and outside the party came on

Prominent anti-Nazis were rounded up and taken to the concentration camp Oranienburg by the SA: leading radio officials and speakers and Social-Democratic party functionaries at the roll-call

June 30, 1934, when he had his old comrade Röhm and many potentially rebellious stormtroopers murdered as well as his old enemies, among them Kahr, Schleicher, and Strasser. Altogether, the SS massacred for Hitler a hundred of his own men and an even larger number of former allies and opponents; only Papen and Hugenberg managed to survive. After that 'night of the long knives', all were dead who might have thwarted his plans. The road was now free for his unopposed dictatorship, for rearmament and aggression, for annexation and war, and for the organized murder of millions.

The *Reichstag* fire has remained something of a mystery. At the time we thought that the evidence pointed clearly to arson by the Nazis. The fact was that the concentration camps were ready, that the stormtroopers had long lists of wanted people whom they took away as soon as the decree of February 28 gave the signal – it was all too well prepared for a mere coincidence just five days before the elections. The event had been timed to achieve its full effect as the funeral pyre of the Weimar Republic.

To be sure, van der Lubbe had been one of the arsonists. But there must have been others; so many points in the building were set alight that a single fire-raiser was unlikely to have done the whole job. Had this simple Dutch Communist been approached by Nazi party officials before the fire, as some sources claimed? Had he been guided into the *Reichstag* through a subterranean passage leading to it from another government building? Who were his helpers, and what happened to them?

At the famous *Reichstag* fire trial in the late autumn of 1933, none of the relevant questions was convincingly answered. Four Communists who had been arrested as fellow-conspirators – the leader of the parliamentary Communist party and three Bulgarians – had to be acquitted. Only van der Lubbe, who throughout the long trial gave the impression of a man drugged into a stupor, was convicted, sentenced to death and executed.

On that bleak February morning after the fire we knew that we were looking at the cinders of the Weimar Republic. It had been a good Republic with a sensible modern Constitution. It would have enabled Germany, if she had only wanted, to rise again in the esteem of the world. As it happened, Berlin alone used that splendid opportunity to the full: it produced a cultural miracle, and within a few years Europe and the whole civilized world received from that single city more stimulation, more new ideas, more faith in the future than from any other cultural community in our century.

Weimar culture was given its special *auto-da-fé* on May 10, 1933 — the burning of the books. On the evening of that day, stormtroopers lit fires in all German towns and threw books that did not conform to National-Socialist thinking into the flames — and this meant practically everything of literary, philosophical, or scientific value published in the Weimar era. In Berlin, Goebbels himself conducted that pseudo-ritual which was aimed at eliminating the spiritual and intellectual vestiges of Germany's most fruitful cultural period.

A hundred and fifty years ago, Heinrich Heine wrote: 'Where men burn books, they will end by burning people.'

The Weimar miracle had been achieved against heavy odds — a vengeful Peace Treaty, the armed rebellions of the first few years of the Republic, the occupation of the Ruhr, inflation, reaction and resentment towards Berlin in the provinces, obstinacy and aloofness of the upper and indifference of the working classes: the momentum of Berlin's 'golden twenties' overcame it all. There was perhaps a chance that, given a few more years, all Germany might have rallied to share the capital's cultural progress.

But then came the international economic crisis with unemployment on an unprecedented scale, demoralization and despair. The political profiteers, the self-seeking tricksters, the murderous paranoics saw their chance, and the ghastly transformation scene began. Why did the sane elements in the German people fail to stop the relapse from culture into barbarism, and with it the plunge into the Second World War? Democracy was a new thing for them, a tender plant that would have needed careful and dedicated nursing. Many 'good' Germans liked to blame the *Ausland*, particularly the western Allies for their own failings. Why didn't the Allies, they asked, stop Hitler on his road to dictatorship? The question itself, which sounds curious to western ears, provides an important clue: it reveals a profound doubt of the Germans in their own responsibility for their government and, by implication, in democracy. I cannot remember any instance of having heard or read in Germany the pronoun 'we' as a collective term including the government as well as the people; the rulers, the authorities are always 'they', especially when there is a question of responsibility or guilt.

The causes of such attitudes, of such traits in the national character, go far back into history, and in Germany's case it was an unfortunate one, a long history of being ruled by innumerable little princes, each an independent authority over his subjects, and no constitutional nonsense. It was they who kept Germany longer than any other major European nation from uniting, from becoming a state; and when this happened at last it was the most militant, the most chauvinistic, the most authoritarian principality of them all that assumed leadership – Prussia. No wonder that the idea of a government by the people was rather alien to the majority of Germans when they were given a chance to make it work by the Weimar Constitution.

Historians are still trying to agree on the reasons why Weimar, with all its cultural achievements, ended as a catastrophic failure. They may find a few clues in an eyewitness account. But even if we knew and understood exactly how and why it all happened, would we act upon our knowledge and understanding in the future? Early in the last century, the German philosopher Hegel wrote, 'What history teaches is that neither peoples nor governments ever learn anything from history.'

SHORT BIBLIOGRAPHY

Peter Bergler, *Rathenau* (Schünemann, Bremen, 1970).

Ronald W. Clark, *Einstein* (Hodder & Stoughton, London, 1973).

Norman Cohn, *Warrant for Genocide* (Eyre & Spottiswoode, London, 1967).

Wolf von Eckardt & Sander L. Gilman, *Bertolt Brecht's Berlin* (Doubleday, New York, 1974).

Erich Eyck, *Geschichte der Weimarer Republik* (Rentsch, Zürich, 1956).

Peter Gay, *Weimar Culture* (Secker & Warburg, London, 1969).

Harold J. Gordon, *Hitlerputsch 1923* (Bernard & Graefe, Frankfurt, 1971).

William Guttmann & Patricia Meehan, *The Great Inflation* (Saxon House, London, 1975).

Wilhelm Hoegner, *Die verratene Republik* (Isar Verlag, Munich, 1968).

Walther Hofer & Christoph Graf, *The Reichstag Fire* (in The Wiener Library Bulletin Nos 35/36, London, 1975)

Thilo Koch, *Die Goldenen Zwanziger Jahre* (Athenaion, Frankfurt, 1970).

Walter Laqueur, *Weimar: A Cultural History 1918–33* (Weidenfeld & Nicholson, London, 1974)

K. Laursen & J. Pedersen, *The German Inflation 1918–23* (North-Holland Publishing Co, Amsterdam, 1964).

Werner Maser, *Adolf Hitler* (Bechtle, Munich, 1971).

Robert Payne, *The Life and Death of Adolf Hitler* (Cape, London, 1973).

John Pritchard, *Reichstag Fire* (Ballantine Books, New York, 1972).

Fritz K. Ringer (ed.), *The German Inflation of 1923* (Oxford University Press, New York, 1969).

Heinz Schmeidler, *Sittengeschichte von Heute* (Carl Reissner, Dresden, 1932).

J. P. Stern, *Hitler: The Führer and the People* (Collins, London, 1975).

Further references to material on the subject are given in the bibliography *From Weimar to Hitler: Germany 1918–1933* published by the Wiener Library in London.

INDEX

188

CROSSCURRENTS *Modern Critiques*

CROSSCURRENTS *Modern Critiques*

Harry T. Moore, *General Editor*